THE FUTURE
OF
INSURANCE

From Disruption to Evolution

Volume III. The Collaborators

Working Together to Move
Insurance Forward Faster

BRYAN FALCHUK
WITH DAVID GRITZ

Insurance Evolution Press

Published by Insurance Evolution Press
Boston, Massachusetts
Copyright © 2023 Bryan Falchuk
All rights reserved. No part of this book may be reproduced, distributed, or transmitted in any form or by any means, including photocopying, recording, or by other mechanical or electronic methods, without the prior written permission of the author, except for use as brief quotations embodied in critical reviews and certain other noncommercial uses as permitted by copyright laws. To request permission, contact the author.

DEDICATION

To all the Insurance professionals willing to question the way we've always done things, and looking to build something better, together.

CONTENTS

FOREWORD FROM SABINE VANDERLINDEN V

THE STORY BEFORE THE STORY BY DAVID GRITZ XI

PREFACE XXIII

I. THE POWER OF COLLABORATION 27
   1. INSURANCE COLLABORATION INDEX 29
   2. BUILD VS. BUY 35
   3. THE ROLE OF THIS BOOK 37

II. WORKING TOGETHER 41
   4. NATIONWIDE & KINETIC 45
   5. MOUNTAIN WEST FARM BUREAU & GUIDEWIRE 59
   6. OHIO MUTUAL & PINPOINT PREDICTIVE 79
   7. AMERICAN EUROPEAN INSURANCE GROUP & PROTOSURE 95
   8. HOMESTEADERS LIFE & BENEKIVA 105

III. COLLABORATING FOR THE FUTURE 123
   9. MAKE FAST, RATIONAL DECISIONS 125
   10. BE ON THE SAME TEAM 131
   11. RESPECT THE LANES OF RESPONSIBILITY 137
   12. EVOLVING AHEAD 141

ACKNOWLEDGMENTS 151

ABOUT THE AUTHORS 155

FOREWORD from SABINE VANDERLINDEN

When I first opened the third edition of the Future of Insurance series, I was struck by the powerful theme of collaboration, as an underlying theme that permeates the very essence of the insurance sector. For over 335 years, the industry has thrived on the principles of exchange, relation, and engagement, even though today's customers often interact with their insurers only a couple of times a year.

As I reflect on my 25 years of experience in the industry, I am privileged to have witnessed the transformative power of digitization and collaboration. While paper-based documentation and face-to-face engagement were once the only recognized, valid form for contracting, today, digital forms of interactions permeate the sector. Throughout my journey, I have encountered established market players and agile insurtechs, all driven by a shared passion for catalyzing change and propelling the industry forward. This dynamic convergence of experience and innovation, wisdom, and unrestrained energy holds the key to unlocking the future of insurance. And as Bryan confesses, the power of collaboration and strategically built partner ecosystems can yield tremendous outcomes. We both have lived on both sides of the equation and learned to appreciate differences between established market players and small entrants while bringing strategic solutions to complex problems.

As we delve into the pages of this book, you will discover the captivating stories of insurance strategists and technologists who are reshaping the industry by harnessing the power of collaboration. You are reminded of the invaluable lessons gleaned from past successes and failures. From embracing the totality of new solutions to fostering agility and open-mindedness, these stories inspire us to learn, adapt, and evolve in the face of uncertainty. They demonstrate that the sector can reinvent itself iteratively and pragmatically to simplify and customize products and services with ease. Each testament reveals that the path to innovation transcends mere technological advancements; it requires a collective effort and an interconnected ecosystem of partners working in unison to create value and redefine the customer experience.

Today's digital landscape is shaping our insurance world somewhat rapidly alongside the emergence of educated and tech-savvy customers, and the relentless pursuit of efficiency and innovation. In this challenging environment, the principle of collaboration has evolved into a harmonious symphony of diverse voices, each contributing their unique expertise and perspective. This unity in diversity enables us to overcome barriers, embrace new possibilities, and drive progress. It also demands that insurance carriers become active participants in the design of solutions, not just the recipients of services.

This book addresses critical questions, such as: How can we collaborate more effectively? Can we innovate in different ways? What benefits does collaboration bring? Can we measure the return on investment from collaboration? These questions can only be answered if we put a different lens on the core concepts of partnership and buy vs. build.

Imagine, if you will, a majestic oak tree standing tall alongside a vibrant, sprouting sapling. The oak provides protection, stability, and wisdom, while the sapling injects fresh ideas and untapped potential into the mix. In this harmonious relationship, they each enhance the other's strengths and counterbalance their weaknesses. This collaboration between tradition and innovation creates a fertile ground where ideas flourish and the best of both worlds merge to birth revolutionary solutions that transform industries.

Such cooperative endeavors pave the way for mutual growth, where established market leaders embrace adaptability and evolution by recognizing the merits and limitations of burgeoning newcomers. Concurrently, these young tech pioneers acquire priceless insights and resources, propelling them to unprecedented heights. This union of diversity is a celebration of collective wisdom and a potent force for progress and innovation in the ever-shifting business landscape.

Capitalizing on state-of-the-art technology, inventive tactics, and a common purpose, these ecosystems of interwoven networks empower members to share ideas, knowledge, and proficiency. This interconnected web cultivates a collaborative culture that fuels imagination, problem-solving, and expansion in the current fast-paced world of digital transformation.

You will find stories between incumbent insurers in the Life and Property & Casualty space with tech companies at various stages of maturity, deploying new solutions while leaning into the startup way to implement.

In the tale of Nationwide and Kinetic, we discover the essential truth of embracing the unknown during the early stages of a solution. This delicate dance between innovation teams and business units paves the way for commercializing ideas, breathing life into them before they wither away. As insurers pirouette to more flexible problem-solving and InsurTechs waltz through industry insights, mutual learning becomes the rhythm that keeps everyone in step. Simplify the choreography by using standard contracts or dividing projects into phases, leaving room for improvisation as the performance unfolds.

Mountain West Farm Bureau and Guidewire's story praises the deployment of technology "as-is", rather than forcing customization upfront. By adopting an iterative test and learn framework, an established player harmonizes with customer needs in no time by ensuring continuous alignment among key stakeholders. Indeed, when it comes to freeing yourself from the shackles of legacy systems, only your best and brightest collaborators will do. The secret is to trust the power of these new solutions, just as you trust the carefully selected partners invested in your success.

Ohio Mutual and Pinpoint Predictive's curious adventure began with a leap of faith into the unknown realm of Artificial Intelligence. Through trial and error, they crafted a process that respected their values and embraced explainability and transparency as part of the core design. By boldly stepping onto the dance floor, they could outmaneuver competitors and seize opportunities in a rapidly evolving business landscape.

American European Insurance Group and Protosure's inspiring journey teaches us the value of risk-taking and innovation. Fear not the shadows of temporary solutions, for the rewards of growth and development, as they often outweigh them. Forge ahead with a right-sized, risk-based strategy, and let your curiosity guide you through the labyrinth of legacy systems to unlock untapped potential.

Lastly, Homesteaders Life and Benekiva remind us of the importance of defining clear responsibilities and nurturing trust. Honesty, humility, and the willingness to listen are the golden threads that bind these relationships together. While partnering with a startup may be risky, the potential cultural benefits can prove to be priceless treasures.

Disruption or evolution? Definitely evolution. As we journey through these captivating stories, remember the wisdom we've gleaned. Embrace learning, prioritize communication, and collaborate in harmony. By doing so, we can all become the conductors of meaningful change in insurance and compose a symphony on innovation supported by an orchestra routed in the diversity of thoughts. It is an honor for all of us to be part of it. The concept of collaboration will morph into unconventional digital ecosystems where we know that the sum of the parts is much greater than each part alone. It is a complex and counter-intuitive concept to grasp as it requires a deep understanding of human behavior and how to build trust with volumes of market constituents. However, honesty and trust can yield more rational decision-making and the allocation of responsibilities among believers of change.

As Bryan concludes, let's help our insurance industry do better. Let's reduce the insularity among companies that could work more effectively together. We are in a collective boat, as everything we do together is interconnected. Maybe the rules we set around us must be questioned for once as we become part of a much larger purpose than ours, whether we build or buy.

– Sabine VanderLinden
CEO & Managing Partner, Alchemy Crew

THE FUTURE OF INSURANCE VOLUME III. THE COLLABORATORS

THE STORY BEFORE THE STORY
by David Gritz

Before we dive into Bryan's traditional case-based analytical approach for the Future of Insurance series, we thought it would be helpful to share a first-hand account of collaboration at work in the insurance industry. Here is my story.

An Outside-In Perspective

As with many insurance insiders, I joined the industry as an outsider. Having spent the early part of my career at Computer Aid (CAI), in corporate IT, I had the opportunity to see how companies across several industries handled technology transformation. CAI was in the business of legacy IT transformation or to use the "dirty" industry word, IT outsourcing. Our primary product was Managed Maintenance, the process of taking over ancient legacy systems built in mainframe, COBOL, or IBM AS/400, and transitioning them to something new. We did this for airlines, state governments, insurers, and utilities.

The actual transition process was painful and required buy-in from the CIO and CFO to make the switch. In the best case, these were healthy transitions where the current staff moved to new applications and value-add projects, while the CAI staff ran the old systems until they were shut down. In the worst case, the transitions were tumultuous and eventually led to mass layoffs. The experience CAI had with chemical companies and airlines since the 1990s is the same experience most insurers are going through now with their digital transformations. Employees are either up to the task of transformation or only capable of turning one crank that might no longer be necessary.

After a year at CAI, I was invited by the CEO to take the role of Director of Partnerships, a role that is becoming popular in the insurance industry. Most insurers have similar roles that go by different names connected to strategy or innovation, but they essentially do the same thing: identify strategies to grow or improve the business through outside partnerships. These could range in type from being with distributors to delivery partners to startup software providers.

The experience of sitting in the partnership seat across multiple industries deeply influenced my perspective on how collaboration can work and why it often fails inside large organizations. It can be a helpful exercise for anyone in insurance to study other industries as most of them have gone through digital transformations in earlier decades.

The Formation of Zero

Flash to 2015, I had had enough time in my corporate role and was ready to spread my wings as an entrepreneur. After several months of discussion, my friend Todd Welch invited me to start an InsurTech that we eventually called Zero for zero lost days of work.

The startup was a spinout of Charter Partners, a captive management company that Todd started. Charter Partners ran a Vermont-domiciled group captive for workers comp and commercial auto risks. The captive participants were primarily blue-collar companies in manufacturing and construction industries ranging from a line-painting company in Souderton, PA to an almond processor in Modesto, CA.

The creation of Zero was in reaction to a major problem with the Charter Partners Captive. Charter Partners was started originally with the vision of bringing together industrial business owners into a collective buying group and mastermind that started with insurance. At its peak, the captive grew to more than 80 members and was trending to $100 million in premium. Everything was going well until it was not.

After a few bad years of loss ratios and a reinsurer bought by private equity, Charter Partners lost its reinsurance contract with only a 30-day notice of non-renewal. From there, chaos ensued. Brokers pulled their clients and placed them with traditional insurers and the captive sunk to less than $10 million in premium. Even once Charter Partners secured a new reinsurer, the business was still running on life support. No one had identified a permanent answer to the high loss ratio.

Until Todd had an idea: the captive members must systematize learning through technology. A systematic learning approach would overcome the traditional forms of loss control and risk management that only have short-lived results. Traditional methods tend to focus on in-person training on specific disciplines of safety and often only reach a small subset of the staff.

The fundamental problem is that training is susceptible to the Ebbinghaus Forgetting Curve. The curve was created in 1885 by Hermann Ebbinghaus to determine how much information individuals retain over time. Following the curve, individuals forget as much as 50% of the new information they learned in one day. Within a week, individuals only retain 20% of what they learned. So, even the best trainers in the world cannot ensure that line workers in a factory remember every safety procedure or can implement it in their job. And most training is not even given to all employees as it would be too expensive, so some never get the chance to forget a safer way of working since they weren't taught it in the first place.

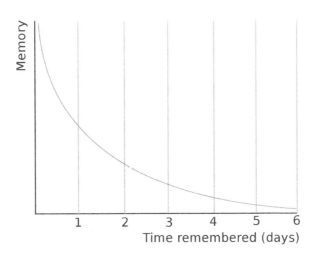

Ebbinghaus Forgetting Curve (Source: Wikipedia)

To combat this fact of human nature, Todd's idea was simple. Build an app that could systematize learning and increase awareness of the risks of the job every day for every employee. Allow information about safety to be shared both down the organization from the plant manager and production staff and up the organization from line workers. Let the best ideas win and store them for the future.

My role at Zero was to bring Todd's idea to reality as the Head of Product. Todd and I worked together to build software that could meet the needs of the captive members and support a broader set of clients in high-risk industries. If it all worked out, we would both fix Charter Partners and have a product that could help industrial companies globally.

Enter Paul O'Neill, Safety Savant
As with any new product, it was necessary to gain a deep understanding of the problem space. After several months of study, we learned that there was no universal standard for safety best practices. Some organizations held annual meetings to review the previous year's performance and major claims. Others held weekly toolbox talks to discuss the dangers of the job. However, none of the companies we interviewed had daily activities to increase awareness and focus on behavior-based safety.

So, we decided to find an expert. While attending the National Safety Council conference, I polled a number of experienced safety managers on who they thought was the hero of industrial safety. The universal answer was Paul O'Neill, former U.S. Secretary of Treasury and CEO of Alcoa. O'Neill is most famous for the 1987 Alcoa shareholders meeting where he suggested safety is more important than shareholder returns. In fact, O'Neill went as far as to say his goal was zero lost days of work at Alcoa. At the time of "greed is good" capitalism, very few shareholders aligned with O'Neill's views.

He proved everyone wrong in his thirteen years as CEO with his financial track record. Over his time in leadership, he increased net income by four-fold and market capitalization by almost 10x. More importantly to the safety community, he reduced the time lost at work due to employee injury by almost 90%. He was a legend.

Not thinking twice, I knew I had to meet O'Neill. So, I sent a cold email to him at his AOL email address. To my surprise, he responded and was willing to talk. After several conversations and a visit to his Pittsburgh office, we persuaded him to be an advisor to Zero and help us drive the vision of the company.

O'Neill brought intellectual heft and a proven operating model to drive safety. Distilling it to its essence, O'Neill's approach focused on three key elements. First, a company must give a voice to all of its employees and empower them to cause change. When he first joined Alcoa, he was famous for touring plants and offering employees his personal home phone number to call and report safety concerns and share ideas. This direct-to-the-CEO channel became a signal that everyone had a voice in the company and that the best ideas could bubble to the top.

Second, a company must eliminate unsafe operations with the same rigor it treats non-value add manufacturing operations. Most manufacturers apply lean and six sigma principles. The beauty of this approach is that sophisticated manufacturing operations already have six sigma and statistical process control methods coded into their business. All they need to do is apply them to safety.

Third, a company must turn operational excellence into a daily ritual. Paul O'Neill's daily ritual was to ensure all staff in his organization could answer Yes to three questions:

1. Am I treated with dignity and respect by everyone I encounter?
2. Am I given the resources I need to make a contribution to the organization that adds meaning to my life?
3. Is my work recognized by someone whose opinion matters to me?

We took O'Neill's ideas and combined them with the lessons from the captive members to build Zero. After about one year of development, we formally launched the application at Sharing Summit, held at Lehigh University in September 2016.

The story of O'Neill is one that should be studied by insurance executives as claims typically make up 65 cents on every premium dollar. So, moving the needle on claims will have a bigger impact than any other single focus area. Also, having unwavering support from the CEO and a simple decision-making framework (e.g., lean principles) can be a powerful force for change. These ideas I learned from O'Neill mirror some of the research Bryan will present in later chapters.

Growth Makes Collaboration a Necessity

Post-launch, we went through many of the same growing pains of most startup companies: closing deals, onboarding clients, and hiring talent.

We installed Zero with many of the captive members and a few outside clients.

As with any growth-oriented startup, we hit an inflection point where we needed additional capital to fund software development and accelerate sales growth. To that point, Todd had personally funded the company. Initially, we planned to raise a Seed Round of one million dollars from angel investors and captive members. Todd and I traveled to Pittsburgh, PA; Modesto, CA; Ewing, NJ; and other small towns to pitch investors. The approach worked to get us verbal commitments for the majority of the raise.

Simultaneously, Todd's brother, Glenn Welch, the Head of Insurance for the captive, worked on raising funds from corporate investors. He initially raised a convertible note from PMA Insurance and started initial negotiations with Everest Insurance for an investment.

The Welch family had a long-standing relationship with executives at Everest Insurance that stemmed back to the Bowers, Schumann & Welch agency started by Todd's father. Glenn's idea was to work with Everest on a more substantial seed investment of five million dollars and an agreement to pre-purchase licenses for Everest clients.

Everest Insurance and Zero

As with most startups, we faced the challenge of having to raise money and operate the business with a relatively meager staff. Added to that, we had a two-track fundraising approach that split our efforts between corporate investors and angel investors.

We faced a crossroads in our fundraising strategy. My preference was to raise less money from angel investors to have more control and less dilution. Todd's preference was to find one good corporate partner that could support our capital needs and help us with sales. After substantial internal debate, we decided to abandon the angel investor route and focus solely on corporate investors.

After we decided, Glenn focused on the Everest relationship while Todd and I worked with the team on product and sales. At first, things seemed to go smoothly. We had an internal sponsor at the divisional president level. Everest brought us into their Liberty Corner, NJ office to meet its CEO and there was excitement all around. However, progress took a turn once we had a verbal commitment.

Days turned to weeks, weeks turned to months, and the pages kept increasing in the agreement. Finally, after more than a year and almost running out of money, we had an over 100-page agreement between Zero and Everest. The agreement covered almost every imaginable scenario, had performance metrics and tranched payments, and featured some restrictions on our ability to work with other insurers. It was almost ready to be signed.

However, one major sticking point remained. How can Everest trust the quality and controls put forth by our offshore development team? Everest was concerned that since our core developers were not in the United States, they may either abandon the project or steal our code.

At the time, we had hired a Philadelphia-based InsurTech, Livegenic, which also offered development services. Although Livegenic was incorporated in the US and its CEO was based in Philadelphia, Livegenic's developers resided in Ukraine. Regardless of the corporate structure, Everest was still concerned since the developers worked for Livegenic and not directly for us.

Todd and I put together a two-part plan to mitigate the risk of the offshore development team. First, I would audit the team to make sure their security and business practices were up to par. Second, we would hire a CTO in Pennsylvania.

Shortly after the decision, I flew off to Kharkiv, Ukraine with Livegenic's CEO, Olek Shestakov. The goal was to visit the office, see how the team worked, and identify any risks. To my pleasant surprise, the office in Kharkiv was nicer than the Livegenic office in Philadelphia, and the team gelled well. It was also a great bonding opportunity for me and Olek. There is no better way to get to know a vendor than to spend a week in a foreign country with one of its executives and share a week of meals together.

Once the first part of the risk mitigation plan was complete, we shifted our focus to the CTO search. With the help of a recruiter, we were able to identify, interview, and hire our CTO, Pavlo Kovalchuk. A key consideration in the process was that Pavlo had to be a native Ukrainian speaker so there would be no communication gap. That was no problem for Pavlo since he was originally from Odesa, Ukraine.

After we had the risk mitigation plan in place, we presented everything to Everest. Everest remained concerned about the risk of the code being stolen by the offshore team and we faced a stalemate.

Time was ticking and we had to get a deal done or we would run out of money. With that pressure, Todd and Glenn agreed to personally indemnify Everest of any risk of having the code stolen, and we signed the deal.

Now that a deal was in place, we could really get to work. Everest assigned their Chief Administrative Officer (CAO), Bill Thygeson, as our primary point of contact and we put together a plan for working together. Everest had agreed to buy a set number of licenses and would allocate them to some of its clients. Additionally, Everest would work with us to introduce Zero into some of their large industrial accounts.

This plan kicked off a mission to build additional support within Everest. Because Thygeson did not have direct control over Everest's clients, we had to start with education. We ran a series of webinars and held in-person presentations to underwriters and then to some of Everest's major brokers.

The challenge that I did not originally anticipate was that Everest did not own its relationships. As with most reinsurers, they are heavily dependent on their brokers to bring them business and the brokers ultimately own the direct relationships with the policyholders.

In my past role at CAI, things were different. CAI salespeople and the CEO, who viewed himself as a salesperson, owned direct relationships with their clients. CAI salespeople and client CIOs had tight relationships, played golf together, and were often close friends. Sometimes CAI even hired retired CIOs to become account executives for their past companies.

At Everest, underwriters owned blocks of business and rarely had direct personal relationships with the risk managers. Instead, they were intermediated by their broking partners. So even if we had an underwriter interested in Zero, we would have to win the secondary interest of that underwriter's brokers to reach the client. In most cases, the brokers were very protective of their clients and saw our project as a novelty to win business instead of a necessity to drive better loss ratio results.

One area within Everest where we did garner strong support was Everest's loss control division. We were able to work closely with the head of loss control to introduce the platform into accounts and gain valuable product feedback from the loss control team directly. The challenge was, as is the case with most insurers, the loss control department did not always have the power to work proactively with accounts. Adding to this, most loss control staff were overstretched already, so it was hard to lean too heavily on them for help in our mission.

As the relationship with Everest evolved, we continued to make incremental progress, but it was slower than the team anticipated from the beginning. To Everest, Zero represented a great solution for its clients. But it was better suited as an integrated R&D department than a partner organization. As a result, Everest acquired the remaining shares of the business. Today, Zero continues to operate as a division within Everest.

For me, going through the experience allowed me to see firsthand the life cycle of an insurtech and insurer partnership from start to finish. I had a chance to live through the good times and the tough times of the startup lifecycle.

Lessons Learned from the Everest Partnership

Going through my experience, there are four lessons I learned that are transferable to other insurtechs going through the experience of partnership:

1. Insurer time scales are slow, and you must often accept this. In most cases, there are limited options to speed up a partnership process and founders must be ready and able to wade through the carrier processes that usually take more than a year.
2. Insurers are risk-averse to most things that are outside of the ordinary. Most insurers are 100+ year-old organizations with established processes and procedures. Those processes have made them profitable and averted harm. Be prepared to address any non-traditional risks of the partnerships including seemingly innocuous or mundane risks like offshore development.
3. Inking a partnership is not the end game, but merely the beginning. After the ink dries, insurtechs must work to build relationships inside their insurer partner in order to have a successful commercial rollout. Most times, the buyer or

champion is only one of the necessary team members to make your partnership work.
4. Senior management support is essential but does not often get the real work done. Although we had the CEO's backing and our champion was a C-Level executive, that was not enough for us to directly access Everest's client accounts. As in most insurers, underwriters own the relationships with the brokers and the end clients. We had to build relationships at various levels in the organization to work through multiple channels to access new clients.

InsurTech NY and the Need for Partnerships

After my time with Zero, I had the opportunity to advise a number of insurtechs and help them think through partnerships. Through this experience, I realized that the struggle to form productive partnerships was nearly universal. Most founders don't have the partnership muscle built prior to starting their companies. And most individuals within carriers asked to carry out a partnership are doing it for the first or second time.

After Zero, I founded InsurTech NY with my business partner, Tony Lew. At its heart, InsurTech NY was created to bridge the gap between insurers and startups through networking and dedicated partnership support. Our first major offering was created to explore that issue.

The year we started InsurTech NY, we did significant research on what services existed to facilitate startup and carrier relationships. On the low-touch side, there were a number of programs called accelerators that were organized by investors or non-profit organizations that followed a cohort model. Accelerators like GIA, Gener8tor, and Lloyd's Lab organized groups of insurers into a collective to select a fixed cohort of companies to participate in a time-bound program. In the programs, early-stage companies, sometimes pre-revenue, were mentored by insurers.

On the high-touch side, established consulting organizations like EY and Capgemini have setup dedicated teams for new product development that have the capability to source insurtechs as part of the delivery process. The EY Nexus program is one example of an offering available to carriers. Consulting company programs are generally focused on projects large enough to warrant the cost of hiring outside help.

However, nothing existed in the middle: a solution that could give high exposure to startups but did not require dedication to a full consulting engagement; a solution that could support existing teams of innovation leaders and not supplant their efforts.

Most insurers have dedicated staff for scouting. Identifying startups can be time-consuming but is not where the value is created. That lies in selecting and partnering with the startups you find. Based on the feedback we received from interviewing more than 40 carriers, we created the InsurTech NY Corporate Innovation Program. It serves as a one-year program dedicated to facilitating partnerships between carriers and startups through structured programming: early-stage discovery; executive round tables; startup showcases; and startup matchmaking.

Through this program, we have been able to work with more than a dozen insurers on the mechanics of partnership from ideation to pilot. These relationships formed the basis for our worldview on insurer-insurtech partnerships.

Now that we have run three cohorts with a total of 80 InsurTech participants and more than a dozen carrier participants, we have had the chance to observe the challenges first-hand in making partnerships work. Startups regularly share with us the difficulty they go through in their partnerships. Many times, major partnership initiatives almost kill the startup and can take up to two years to complete a baseline rollout.

A startup partnership that is stuck in limbo is not good for a carrier either. Carriers need to demonstrate the return on investment of their innovation efforts and make forward progress toward their digital or other initiatives. As I learned from my experience at CAI, most insurers are nearly a decade or more behind other industries and do not have more time to waste or risk falling further behind.

As a result, Tony and I knew we had to do more to support partnerships. Developing research and a worldview behind what we were learning anecdotally was the next logical approach. Forming a worldview or philosophy of how to do something is very much like a scientific theory. You can form a hypothesis, but without testing it against a statistically significant set of data, you cannot validate the hypothesis.

As a result, Tony and I knew that we needed data to validate our approach. Internal debate on how to do this led to a discussion with other consultants, analysts, and thinkers on the topic. Eventually, we determined we needed to form a group to explore this topic and conduct research that could be published and support our business.

Bryan Falchuk was one of the first people we contacted to be part of this research project, which ultimately culminated in the creation of this book.

Now to Bryan.

PREFACE

While it may seem different from the prior two books in the series, this volume is the next logical step in an attempt to move the minds of an industry.

In the first two books, I shared first-hand examples of insurers, old and new, pushing through the barriers we all face in the industry that hold us back from innovating and evolving our products, services, customer experience and the opportunities available to us all. Like a self-help book, the idea was to share stories that look and feel like situations we all may face and show how someone else got through that challenge to move ahead. Through the eyes of others, we can often discover paths to achieve something greater for ourselves, so these stories served to give us all the inspiration to make this possible in our context.

Aside from the inspiration in each story, overarching lessons emerged across stories from both legacy and startup insurers, and these lessons proved to span the divide between old and new, and even apply to others in and around the insurance ecosystem – whether you're a carrier, solution or service provider or something else.

The idea that the lessons from legacy players can apply to startups, and vice versa, started to introduce the notion that perhaps the divide between the two is not so absolute, and there is potential to learn from and work together for the greater benefit of the industry and greater impact for anyone involved in the effort than they could achieve on their own.

That is the genesis for this third book – to continue to teach through real world examples and show how we need not think about other players as separate to us, but potential extensions of our organization. By finding ways to come together and collaborate, we can exponentially increase the art of the possible.

When you think about the purpose of the insurance industry, you understand why it is imperative that we work together to do better than we could on our own. We are here not just to put lives back together when tragedy strikes, but to keep the risks of those tragedies from stopping people from pursuing their dreams, personally and in their business. While we can serve people well on our own, or through the approaches we've used for centuries, with such high stakes, if we can find better ways to work together for that purpose, we should.

One more note on how this book is different from the prior two in the series – it has noticeably fewer case studies in it. That is an unfortunate function of the nature of the book. The prior books had 15 cases between them, and this book has only a third of that. There are several reasons, but the biggest factor is that many insurers do not openly talk about what solution providers they work with or are customers of. Participating in this book would mean being open about that, precluding several interested insurers from ultimately agreeing to share their story. Some offered to share without saying who their company was, but a guiding principle of this series is that the stories must be open and honest. It matters who the companies are, what they did and how it went, so I prioritized giving you transparency and completeness over having more cases that were potentially harder to connect with and learn from.

As a result, the five cases here are honest stories of the ups and downs, roadblocks, challenges, surprises and wins from insurers and their partners, told from first-hand research with the people you will read about in the stories and with the full cooperation and willingness of the companies they represent.

With that, let's begin on the path to the industry finding better ways to work together.

I. THE POWER OF COLLABORATION

The insurance industry has spent billions on innovation, with a clear ramping up of its efforts as it met the imperatives imposed by COVID lockdowns and seized on opportunities created by new solutions brought to market by insurtechs. I wrote about some of these investments in the first and second volumes of *The Future of Insurance*, where we saw how legacy and startup insurers were pushing the industry forward.

And yet, while many of these efforts can be deemed successes, the path to bring them to market has not always been smooth. Indeed, for every successful and smooth implementation, there are no doubt countless others that run over budget, deliver a constrained scope, or fail to see the expected impact and returns materialize. And while the industry has gotten faster in decision making and implementation around new solutions, it is still not fast relative to many other industries. The rule of thumb is that it takes 18 months to bring a new solution to market, but there are many new initiatives that can take multiples of that time.

With this concern in mind, a group of professionals from across the industry came together in 2021 to try to expose and understand what makes collaborations between insurtech solution providers and insurers more or less successful, and what actions and investments the industry can make to ensure we maximize and reap the rewards of our efforts to modernize, innovate and evolve.

This group created the Insurance Collaboration Index (ICI), which uses an anonymous survey of insurtech solution providers to try to understand what makes for better or worse, smoother or rougher collaborations to bring solutions to market. Nearly 150 providers answered a series of questions on different insurers they worked with, scoring how things went at various stages of the project, shedding light on what trends exist between efforts that were deemed a success and those that were more problematic or failures.

Through this research, we learned a lot about what makes for easier or harder projects and what can increase the likelihood of success for the solution provider and the insurer.

Some of our findings were to be expected, such as the level of commitment of resources like a project manager and executive sponsor the insurer was willing to make, while others were more surprising, like that onerous due diligence processes did not impact how collaborative and successful the efforts were in the end.

While we will see some of the key findings in depth here, this book uses case studies to bring more detail to the nuances within the lessons learned from the Insurance Collaboration Index. By shedding greater light on what leads to more or less fruitful collaboration, the lessons from these cases can help insurers and insurtech partners work better together to speed time to market, increase the impact of their innovative efforts, improve customer and employee satisfaction, and help spark a continuous energy of improvement and growth across their organization.

Let's start by reviewing the ICI, and the key findings from it.

1. The Insurance Collaboration Index

A working group comprised of industry veterans was convened in 2021 by InsurTech NY co-founders, David Gritz and Tony Lew, including myself, Alan Walters (formerly of Conning), Cynthia Hardy and Krishnan Venkatachalam of Pivot Global Partners, Mark Gardella of Zephyr Innovation Advisors, Irene Yang of Finesse Innovation, Roi Hansraj of RCI and Mike Fitzgerald (formerly of CB Insights).

We created a survey instrument to gather first-hand, anonymous feedback from insurtech solution providers on their experience working with different carriers to find what drives success (or failure). We learned about how different carriers resourced projects, worked through due diligence, funded their efforts, gave support from senior sponsors and more. We were able to correlate performance on these various sub-dimensions to the overall sense of success in bringing a solution to market.

Insurtechs shared feedback on carriers of differing sizes, market segments, product offerings and geographies. The solutions they worked with those carriers to deliver also spanned a wide range of offerings from back-office technologies to customer-facing products and tools.

We sought feedback on eight major factors that impacted how collaborative efforts went:

Factor	Description
Executive Sponsorship	Effectiveness and engagement of the executive sponsor
Decision Making	Speed and effectiveness of decision making
Definition of Success	Clearly defined success metrics for the partnership
Budget/Funding	Adequate budget for the initiative
Issue Resolution	Ease and completeness of issue resolution
Business & IT Alignment	Alignment of the business and IT on goals, priorities, scope, and business outcomes
Due Diligence	Difficulty or onerousness of due diligence
Resources	Adequate and appropriate resource allocation to the initiative

We asked providers how important they felt each of these factors was, and how they think insurers performed at delivering to those expectations of what's needed for a successful collaboration. We found some potential misalignment between importance to success in the eyes of solution providers and how insurers performed on these factors. This helped to shed light on the potential sources of complications or trouble in a partnership, and where to focus our efforts for improvement going forward.

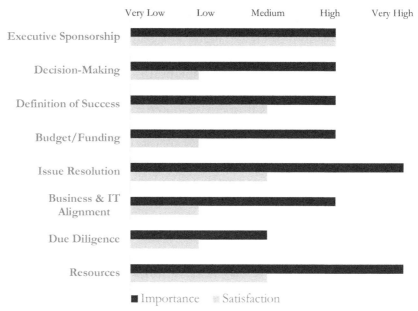

For example, insurtechs rated Executive Sponsorship as being highly important, and gave insurers credit for the commitment leaders showed to the projects they supported. Conversely, having alignment between IT and the business was also deemed as highly important, yet insurtechs saw this as an area carriers should focus on improving further.

However, we sought to move past perceived misalignment on what matters and work to find connection to actual performance. To that end, we looked for what factors were more or less correlated to the success of the initiative to find what really matters to successful collaborations. We all have *ideas* of what we would like from a partner, and we may be right. Perhaps what *truly* helps has eluded both solution providers and insurers, and we all could benefit from learning this to unlock better outcomes all around.

Across all the variety of players and projects, and the different factors we looked into, several things rose to the top as being most impactful on the success of the initiative.

We also found some surprising revelations that may go against what you would expect to be helpful to a project's success but actually don't matter as much.

Let's look at the major findings from the initiative.

Keys to Successful Collaboration

The single most important and highly correlated factor when it comes to what carriers can do to help ensure success when working with an insurtech on implementing a new solution is seemingly obvious, yet frustratingly not done consistently or sufficiently. Based on feedback we received, that thing is properly resourcing the project. This factor was strongly correlated to the success of a project, with a correlation coefficient of nearly 0.75. This is also an area where expectations and performance do not align in the discussion and chart above.

'Properly resourcing a project' is a broad term that can take on many specific meanings, but the extent to which carriers assigned dedicated resources to oversee a project, engage in a pilot or proof of concept (PoC), train staff on how to use the tools, have technical staff working on API connections, etc., can make or break a project.

For example, a carrier may assign a project manager to oversee implementation, but that person may not be committed to the project, invested in its success, or have the bandwidth to really stay on top of its delivery. Or there may be an assigned resource, but the person assigned gets swapped out several times, so it's still a dedicated resource on paper, but not in practice. I have also seen many projects that go well up until the pilot phase where carriers fail to assign pilot users to get genuinely involved, instead rotating people through or letting them skip meetings or not bother engaging with the solution if they're busy or disinterested.

The second-most impactful thing a carrier can do to ensure success may seem odd as it sounds like it implies that things are failing already. Invariably, even the best projects hit bumps in the road, whether that be delays, complications, surprise developments or worse. According to survey respondents, it's not *whether* you keep problems from arising, but how you respond when they do that matters.

Specifically, having communication and decision-making protocols and pathways clearly defined so that issues can be raised, discussed, and resolved quickly was nearly as important as having dedicated resources, with a correlation to success only one-one-hundredth below resourcing (0.74).

For example, many carriers have well-established protocols to address problems, but they may require fitting a meeting cadence or timing that draws out project timelines or risks scope and budget. Having a more flexible and responsive path to ensure time isn't lost or the opportunity to manage the negative impact of problems isn't missed can be a crucial differentiator between projects that flounder and those that thrive.

Put together, carriers can setup project teams with resources that are committed and engaged in the success of the project and have well-established pathways to resolve issues and overcome barriers as they arise so that they can be addressed quickly and completely.

Surprising Findings on What Doesn't Help

While these factors are still correlated with success, there are some that you may expect to be highly correlated yet have less direct impact in practice, if any. Specifically (and surprisingly), having sufficient budget is *not* highly correlated with success. That is, innovation and successful InsurTech deployments are more dependent on *how* you engage by dedicating people to the project and working to resolve issues than to *how much money* you are willing to spend.

This was a very interesting finding as many carriers assume that innovation is expensive, or that they may lack the budget to be innovative. We often hear about nine-figure system projects in the industry (and the struggles they face despite their huge budgets), and that scares many carriers away from innovation.

On the contrary, how you use the resources you have is much more important than the scale of resources at your disposal. You will see this play out in some of the stories here where creative deployments of budgets with strong execution won the day.

A corollary to this is that you cannot make up for a lack of committed resources or a difficult or unhelpful issue resolution process with money. That is, paying the insurtech to solve the problems or spending more on systems integrators (SIs) was not found to save troubled projects, while dedicated resources and effective internal issue resolution at the carrier was.

Another interesting finding in terms of what *isn't* tied to success is the complexity and time-intensity of due diligence. After hearing many insurtechs complain about arduous or onerous due diligence reviews with carriers, and having had to grind through many myself, you might think that these can completely or at least significantly derail projects or hinder their progress toward success. Instead, while insurtechs may not appreciate particularly slow or difficult due diligence processes, they noted that project work often continued in parallel, and, eventually, they got through the review.

So, while you must have sufficient budget for the project and shouldn't make due diligence harder than it truly needs to be, spending more or forgoing asking the questions you need to ask won't lead to greater chances of success in working with an insurtech to innovate in and evolve your business.

What May Seem Obvious Isn't Always

While it may seem obvious that having dedicated resources and removing barriers quickly and effectively can keep a project on track, in practice, we find that judging performance here mirrors what the industry learned around customer experience – it's not how *you* judge yourself, but how those you work with judge you.

The Insurance Collaboration Index was a unique and rare opportunity for carriers to get real, unfiltered insight into how they're performing, and where to focus their energy to be more effective and efficient with their innovation efforts.

Beyond the insights discussed above, one of the biggest learnings from this work is the need for carriers to seek honest feedback from their partners so they can learn how to do better, just like we seek to do with our insureds and trading partners. And the same is true in the other direction, with carriers needing to give open, honest feedback to their solution providers and partners. We may not always like what we hear, but we can always learn and grow from it, and that will serve to make us more effective in future efforts to move our business forward.

Getting that feedback can be hard. Those selling to us may not want to be as honest as they need to be for fear of losing our business. Those we sell to may not want to offend us or may need our help in the future, and don't want to risk awkwardness or poor service as a punishment for sharing something they wished was better.

Despite these barriers, there are ways to learn how we can improve. One way is through the eyes of our peers, by hearing their stories and the lessons within them. That is why this book was an obvious next step in the journey we began with the ICI – to bring first-hand, honest stories of collaboration to the industry so we can all learn and grow.

2. Build vs. Buy

It would be hard to talk about collaboration between insurtechs and insurers without acknowledging that some carriers choose to do things themselves, making this entire discussion seem to be a moot point. This would be a flawed assumption for two reasons.

First, increasingly, insurers are looking outside for solutions they have historically built themselves. This is driven by an explosion of lightweight, API-connected point solutions and a move to the cloud. Having a wealth of ways to solve problems we face and implement them more readily makes the decision to look outside much more palatable.

And this presumes we're talking about using an external solution to replace a home-grown system or tool. In fact, many of the things carriers are looking for solutions for were solved using people or offline workarounds. That is, there was no system-based solution in place yet as technology had not gotten to a level where it could meet our needs. So, sometimes 'build' wasn't even something we actually built.

This has been changing rapidly. Historically human-based or offline ways of working now have viable digital alternatives that are more efficient, power our efforts to get better data to feed into our decision-making models and provide a more seamless customer experience.

Second, just because you may still opt to build something yourself, doesn't mean you can't benefit from lessons of collaboration from situations where a solution is bought from an external partner. To build something requires similar resources, structures, and processes to buying something, it's just that we happen to sit on both sides of the equation instead of only one.

In some ways, this can be a positive since we can control all aspects of the work, which is a main reason some insurers choose the 'build' approach. This can lessen the burden to be effective collaborators because we're all on the same team.

In other ways, it can be a negative because everyone is subject to the same constraints, like culture and politics, making how we collaborate perhaps even more critical. And, despite everyone being from the same company, we may not feel like we are actually on the same team. Ask yourself if IT is referred to as a person in your company, like, "IT said we can't do XYZ," or, "IT made us use this new tool." I know I've certainly seen this situation many times myself, but have yet to meet this person named "IT".

It also robs us of the chance to learn from others with different ways of looking at problems and approaching solutions. We often get glimpses of this when we hire someone from outside our company or team, and benefit from their new perspective. Collaborating with an outside partner presents a chance to learn and grow over and above whatever solution we end up with in the end that we would miss if we had built the solution ourselves. This comes up in one of the cases in this book specifically.

Build vs. Buy will continue to be debated in our industry and others for years to come, if not indefinitely. And it should be. There is no single right answer for all situations, contexts, and companies. But regardless of what you answer for your situation, being an effective Builder or Buyer depends on how you work together, what decisions you make, the resources you have to work with, how you use them, etc.

The insights from the ICI and the cases in this book still apply, regardless of whether the insurtech solution provider you use for your next project works for the same company as you or not.

3. The Role of This Book

Previous books in this series share the stories of insurers moving part of their business forward, or, in the case of the startups, the creation and building of their business overall. Through their stories, you can take lessons on how to innovate in and evolve your business.

This book is a bit different.

Rather than looking at a single company in each case or digging into the specifics of the thing they were building, we will look at the coming together of two companies in each case and how that went. While we will talk about some solutions and what they can do, it's more important here to investigate *how they did it* to see what we can all learn about approaching change collaboratively.

Each story has unique nuances to it, with challenges and successes that are interesting and may or may not resonate with you or your situation. Hearing about these things in varied contexts and seeing how different companies navigate them can inspire us all to relook at our own situation and find ways to do better.

While the cases are hopefully interesting reads in their own right, it is important that we all see the lessons within those stories. To help with this, you will find key takeaways at the end of each case, called, "Foundations for the Future," as has been done with all other books in this series. Some of those insights will be sudden and readily apparent, and some will develop slowly as the story unfolds. That means as you read, you may not see sudden moments of insight, but will take in very interesting stories of journeys in changing the industry that develop lessons as they play out. I will try to draw your attention to insights or critical realizations throughout but will call them out specifically at the end of each case story.

Spending time reflecting on these lessons, how they were exhibited in the case itself, and whether you might see something similar in your own world can help us find ways to do better every day.

And, just like the rest of the series, the final section of this book will pull together the overarching themes that are present across the cases so you can take the meta learnings from all of these stories into your own world to help you move forward.

You should walk away from this book with a clearer sense of what it can take for insurers and insurtechs to work effectively together to bring change and progress to this industry. This book can help inform your sense of how to work together more effectively, what that might take from your side, and what you should look for from the other side.

With that, let's start the journey through these five stories of collaboration:

- Nationwide & Kinetic
- Mountain West Farm Bureau & Guidewire
- Ohio Mutual Insurance Group & Pinpoint Predictive
- American European Insurance Group & Protosure
- Homesteaders Life & Benekiva

II. WORKING TOGETHER

Here, we explore the journeys of five insurers and their partners with different goals, cultures, past failures and successes. For some of the stories, they are far earlier in their journey, so there will no doubt be more to learn from them as time goes on. For others, the outcome of their collaborative efforts are in full swing, delivering on the value they hoped to unlock together and more. For one, their relationship is set to wind down, as expected when they first came together. And for some, the partnership developed spans both commercial and investment relationships, adding additional nuances to their journey together.

Despite their differences, what remains the same across all of these efforts is the desire to not only solve a specific problem or meet a specific market need, but to move both organizations forward. Equally, everyone in these stories had ideas about what would work best (or not) combined with a clear recognition that they may not know everything and should maintain a willingness to be open to the ideas of others.

If you look into these stories, you find the advice of the prior books present. Customer and employee focus and engagement still matter, as does having clarity on what you're trying to achieve and staying true to that. Each company here chose to work together for the challenge and growth they would gain by combining different mindsets, skills and approaches to their efforts, knowing the power of diversifying their thinking. Whether the story involves direct investment or investment through spending on a commercial implementation, the role of capital is ever present here as it was with the prior books. Lastly, it is apparent that none of the players in this story were interested in being an also-ran, but rather finding material advantage through their efforts so they could truly thrive.

Like the prior books, it's important to remember that these insurers and insurtechs aren't unique. While they may seem different from each other or from whatever you face, the decisions and challenges they have to navigate could easily occur in any context. Some pieces of their journey may not resonate for many of you, but if you look deeper, you will likely see an analog to your situation so you can learn and grow from their experience. As before, this is part of why I have chosen very different stories, market segments and situations so that, when the stories are taken together, it is hard for anyone to say nothing could apply to their world. All of this is to reinforce that there are challenges in and learnings to take from all situations – a tenet I have stressed in my work for years.

There is no explicit, universal blueprint in this book intentionally because one does not exist. What we all must do is translate what we observe to our situation in a humble and honest way, look for where we can break old habits, challenge whether we can do better, and find moments to move our business ahead through the work we get to do with others. These stories are shared to inspire you about the journey and what you can bring into your own path.

Outside of this series, I have also written a series of personal development books. One in particular, *The 50 75 100 Solution*, is about how we change relationships fraught with conflict. The overarching theme is, whether or not we are the source of the problem, we can be the source of the solution. That is the advice I would give all of you to hold dear as you read these stories and think about what they mean in your situation.

Whether we blame the other party for a failed project, there could always be things we could do differently to affect a better outcome. That takes a level of willingness to challenge your own choices that many of us struggle to have. Therefore, I raise this point explicitly to help prime you to take as much potential value from these stories as possible – something that can only come if you're willing to look at yourself or your organization.

And while you may think the cases here are all examples of perfect collaborations, within them you will find plenty of tough moments, challenges, and conflict (both internal and external). That is only to serve as more fodder for lessons to be taken, and to remind us that even those we may look to as successes can suffer from the same cultural difficulties as anyone else. The key to their success is in their willingness to choose to do differently from how they have in the past. That is a choice each of us can make.

It can be hard, but it's still a choice.

I encourage you to take notes, think about your specific context, consider how each case might apply to it, and reflect on how the learnings and takeaways can impact what you hope to achieve or perhaps inspire an idea for something new entirely.

Talk about what you've read with a colleague, peer or your boss and challenge each other to see how you can evolve your world regardless of what you face or where you are starting from.

With that, let's begin our journey with Nationwide Insurance and Kinetic.

4. Nationwide & Kinetic

Growing up in the UK in the 1990s and 2000s, Haytham Elhawary witnessed something that would shape his future in ways he could not yet comprehend. The son of an elder care nurse, Elhawary would see his mother come home from work injured on a regular basis. Constant bending, rotating, lifting, and straining takes a toll on people. And when those actions come when you're caring for others, you often set aside the impact on yourself to be sure you give those in your care what they need.

Elhawary's mother had to work through the pain, often only making things worse. Of course, when she came home, she had a family to care for regardless of her condition, making it harder and harder for her to get on the other side of her repeated injuries and exhaustion. When those injuries were too great to work through, it would impact her ability to help support her family.

This story is not unique to Elhawary's mother or family, nor to the work of nurses and other first responders. The pattern repeats itself in many physical jobs like manufacturing, logistics, janitorial services and maintenance, food production and more.

Watching his mother go through this on a regular basis was hard enough but seeing her loaded onto an ambulance one day when she could not move due to a pulled muscle that kept getting worse and worse, Elhawary knew he had to do something. As a child, he wanted to help his mother. That set him on a path of curiosity and study, leading him to get a master's in engineering and a PhD in robotics. With his expertise in mechanics and physics, he knew the problem was much bigger than he original thought, and so the solution needed to be, too.

This was the genesis for the idea behind Kinetic, a company Elhawary co-founded with CTO Aditya Bansal in 2014 with a mission to reduce workplace injuries at scale. Their goal was and still is to reduce the most prevalent musculoskeletal injuries, like sprains and strains, amongst those doing manual labor, like workers in construction, housing, healthcare, hospitality, warehouses and more. Elhawary said, "If we can reduce sprain and strain injuries, we're impacting the most prevalent, hard-to-recover-from injuries in the population more broadly."

To do this, Kinetic spent a year and a half developing a small wearable device that measures how the body moves and uses a vibration to signal to the wearer that they were moving in a way that increased their chance of injury. This last part is the key to delivering on Kinetic's mission. Many solutions can observe movement and give you information in a dashboard or app to reflect on later and think about what you could do differently going forward. But to be able to tell you in the moment so you can stop before it's too late is the unlock to preventing injuries, not just learning from those we ended up with.

This is what caught the eye of Erik Ross of Nationwide Ventures in 2016 when he was at a Workers Compensation and Safety conference where he saw Elhawary and Kinetic. As the venture investment arm of an insurer, they were interested in solutions that could reduce injuries and other types of losses but found that most of what they saw lacked what they called an 'action layer' – the ability to intervene and stop the injury rather than just report on it later.

Given the strong impression Elhawary and the action layer solution Kinetic was creating had on Ross, he brought Brian Anderson from the Ventures team in on the idea so he could look more closely at Kinetic to see if it might be worth investing in. Anderson was immediately intrigued by the ability to proactively reduce loss frequency and severity, saying, "Many wearables can understand something, but they can't get you to *do* something. They miss that action layer. Kinetic had the solve here because it can intervene rather than just report later."

The investment team found what Kinetic was doing to be very intriguing and spent the next few months digging in deeper on the concept, the team and the potential of making an investment. It was important to not just test the actual solution itself to ensure its viability, but Anderson shared the importance of the culture at Kinetic, the fast pace of positive change in their offering, and the company's vision and mission.

While Nationwide is not a market share leader in Workers Compensation (WC), they wanted to be sure there was a strong loss prevention story driving companies they invest in as they seek investments that align with Nationwide's core business. Since ending worker injury was the impetus behind its founding going back to Elhawary's childhood, Kinetic felt like a good strategic fit for Nationwide to invest in.

For some insurance corporate venture capital (CVC) teams, they specifically want their insurance business to be a customer of the investment. With less of a presence in Workers Compensation than in other lines, and within that, a focus outside of the target classes of business for Kinetic, it wasn't clear that Nationwide itself could become a customer or partner of Kinetic. Even if it could, the venture arm generally is able to move faster than the business, so rather than waiting to see if there was a commercial application with investment targets, Nationwide Ventures tends to lead with an investment before a commercial implementation can take place.

That was the case here, with the venture team investing only four months after first meeting the Kinetic team at that conference. Kinetic was not actively raising a round at the time but was able to issue a convertible note to Nationwide, which provided the startup additional runway.

As many investors will tell you, building hardware is hard. It takes a lot of time and money to develop, and hardware meant for industrial settings is even tougher because of the need to battle test your equipment and invest in the durability of it. It is also hard to get investment in industrial solutions like this as much of the venture world is focused on software and B2C applications, with less understanding and interest in the gritty world that is industrial tech. Add in the complexity of hardware, and getting investors is even trickier.

Kinetic learned these lessons first-hand. They had done six prototype iterations when Nationwide Ventures was first interested, which was the limit of what their existing angel funding would support. They had also run some small pilots, and could see the potential, but needed more experience and data. The between-round funding from Nationwide allowed them to move forward on two critical components – pilots and proof of value – that would be critical to reaching the next phase for the company.

With the investment in place, Nationwide Ventures wanted to help Kinetic refine the idea and identify potential commercial applications. Anderson introduced the team to leaders in Nationwide's Workers Compensation team. This gave Kinetic access to strong knowledge champions within the business, which is critical to navigating the process of bringing something new to market. It was helpful to have the venture team supporting them, but they would need leaders within the business itself to go to the next level – commercialization.

The two companies identified some customers to run pilots in, giving Kinetic additional real-world data, and giving Nationwide's underwriting function a chance to learn about the impact of wearables on their exposures.

The pilots were in the trucking space, which proved to be less of a fit for Kinetic's solution than either side hoped for, but there did not seem to be better applications within Nationwide's existing book at the time. Because they were still early in their journey, the team at Kinetic had not yet gotten clarity on the right kind of customer for their solution. Because injuries Kinetic was designed to impact were not the main root causes of injuries for the pilot insureds, it was hard to get these companies to really buy into the solution and adopt it enough to drive insights. That made the pilots less successful than either side would have wanted, and meant it was not a main focus for Nationwide's WC team. Clearly, there was a product-market fit issue here.

Adding to this, the WC team changed at Nationwide, and the champions Kinetic had been working with moved on, leaving Kinetic without key supporters in the business.

Kinetic did not put all of their commercialization eggs in Nationwide's insurance basket, though, and was also investing in pilots with other types of businesses. They found a strong story with large, self-insured companies like Frito-Lay, Oshkosh, Iron Mountain and others. While this brought in revenue, it also gave Kinetic clarity on who their market is, and what the efficacy and impact of their device and the safety dashboard they built around it can be. This helped them to not only intervene pre-injury but identify training needs and risk issues to be addressed from the behavioral patterns their solution was observing.

They spent the next three to four years selling into these larger organizations, growing their business and amassing more and more injury data. This enabled Kinetic to solve for a major hurdle with any loss prevention solution – proof that it prevents losses, and that the value of those losses more than pays for the solution.

Armed with historical loss data from their large customers, Kinetic engaged actuarial consulting firm Perr&Knight in 2021 to validate and size the impact of their solution. P&K found that sprain and strain injuries were reduced by 55% with Kinetic's solution in place, and lost days were reduced by 73%. For anyone who has worked in this space, you know that these kinds of improvements are nearly unheard of, and the fact that these results can be achieved through a simple wearable that vibrates when you are at risk is even more impressive.

With this actuarial proof, Kinetic started to approach insurers to offer their solution alongside WC policies. Because the idea was novel, the point of entry into carriers was generally the innovation group. Kinetic would do a pilot, see great results, and then nothing would happen.

Elhawary recalls, "This was because there was often a disconnect between the innovation team and the business leaders, making it very hard to really embed it in the business in production."

Seeing the true value in their offering rather than just being an add-on to an insurance carrier's offering, they decided they needed to solve for the insurance part of the equation themselves and start an MGA. This is reminiscent of Beam Dental's story in *Volume II* of this series, where dental insurers were not interested in taking the next step with Beam's connected toothbrush despite the clear actuarial benefit of the solution, so Beam started their own dental insurer.

Actually, Kinetic did not come to this conclusion on their own as they didn't even know what an MGA was yet. Nationwide Ventures had continued to invest in Kinetic through subsequent funding rounds, and, as such, had a seat at the table for strategic debates like the one the company was having at that time. Hearing about the struggles with existing carriers and knowing the impact Kinetic could have on the return on capital for a WC insurer, they raised the idea of using the MGA model as a solution. This would allow Kinetic to create a product, engage in loss prevention and reap the rewards of the positive outcomes it had proven it could generate without facing the capital requirements of funding a full-stack carrier.

Kinetic started talking to fronting carriers to back their MGA and found very different responses based on the profile of the carrier.

While almost all carriers were interested (though Kinetic did get one flat out refusal), the offerings varied based on the extent to which the carrier had an existing presence in WC. Carriers with more mature WC books could offer Kinetic more operational support, yet they were also apprehensive because of the fear of competing with or cannibalizing their existing book. Some of these carriers also had such established WC businesses that they offered fairly fixed operating models to Kinetic, which wasn't necessarily what would work best for the startup. And those without much of a WC business were not necessarily able to support Kinetic enough.

What really set the carriers apart was this second issue around the level of support they could offer, and how much flexibility they would allow Kinetic. This would be important to Kinetic as they needed to learn and adjust as they went forward since so much of what they were doing had never been done before. Any partner who locked them into too tight of a box would not be a good fit and could make the program less successful.

With an introduction from the Ventures team, Kinetic met with Nationwide's Excess & Surplus (E&S) unit as a potential capacity provider, which is where programs sit. The E&S business came to Nationwide through acquisition and is run out of a different headquarters (Scottsdale, Arizona). Because of that, the E&S team wasn't familiar with Kinetic, despite the venture investment and engagement the startup had in the main headquarters in Columbus, Ohio. An introduction from Anderson was helpful, but there was no sense that the E&S team *had* to offer capacity to Kinetic just because Nationwide was an investor.

Dale Hoppe is the Vice President of Workers Compensation Programs at Nationwide E&S and was the lead executive looking at potentially backing Kinetic's MGA. Elhawary re-pitched the concept to Hoppe in 2021, adding in the proposed MGA business to the original concept Nationwide Ventures had been involved with so far.

Once they knew they were going to setup an MGA, Kinetic starting hiring and building out key capabilities they would need to make that happen, including hiring a Head of Underwriting, setting up the necessary subsidiary structure, getting licensed in 50 states and more. This shortened their runway, but they decided they needed to have these things in place to be able to move the moment they had capacity. They also found it to be important in their dealings with insurers as it added more validity to their proposal. Many new MGA proposals are just ideas, if not almost promises. Kinetic could show material actions and concrete underwriting results through their actuarial study from P&K.

This stood out to Hoppe and Nationwide, who offered capacity to Kinetic along with an attractive mix of what Kinetic could control and what Nationwide would provide operationally. Kinetic would underwrite and control distribution, while Nationwide would provide claims, billing, regulatory compliance, capacity and reinsurance.

This seemed like a good mix, with one exception that I questioned – the decision not to use existing distribution relationships Nationwide had so Kinetic could hit the ground running. Elhaway was clear on why they decided to do it themselves. He said, "We realized through early pilots and our own selling of the solution that the educational burden was too high to piggyback on an existing broker network. If you outsource distribution, you are too far from why people buy – or don't buy. We had to do this part ourselves."

With an agreement to move ahead together on the MGA in the summer of 2021, Kinetic set a goal of writing business by January 1st, 2022 – an aggressive timeline for a totally new MGA. And, despite agreeing to move ahead, there was no contract in place, let alone systems, training, processes, etc. It was clear they would need to find ways to accelerate the entire process to hit a target date less than six months away.

Speeding this up started by working with a very standard MGA agreement, and not trying to negotiate or change much. Another hurdle for a startup would come in due diligence, where Kinetic would have to provide their financials. This concerned them since, as a tech startup, they had been running at a loss since they started in 2014. However, since Nationwide was an investor in the business, that was not a surprise, and the Ventures team could help the E&S team understand and get comfortable with the financial profile of a scaling, technology-based business. Internal partnership and communication between Nationwide Ventures and the E&S business was critical here.

Kinetic also benefitted from Nationwide not having a large Workers Compensation presence, which could have slowed things down as the two sides would have to work through potential conflicts or how to draw lines around how to coexist as competitors.

Systems would also be critical to success on both sides and presented a potential choke point. Nationwide's IT procedures have clearly defined processes and timelines for extending system access to partners or implementing new products or technology. And because this was mid-year, there would be other projects and priorities in flight already that Kinetic would have to get in line behind. Because of the tight timelines and Nationwide's existing investment (and the time the Ventures team had spent making the company aware of Kinetic already), Hoppe was able to get an exception from IT to give Kinetic system access in a few days instead of the standard 30.

Aside from good internal relationships and communications, two other factors contributed to this speed on the IT front. First, because the E&S business operates outside of the core P&C business, their systems are a bit less involved or interdependent than those of the 'mothership' business. Changes to the E&S systems are inherently smaller, with less potential to impact other parts of the company, which made it easier for IT to take action quickly here.

> "The risk right now is about whether the market wants it, and then we can invest in doing it more smoothly."
>
> – Haytham Elhawary
> Co-Founder & CEO,
> Kinetic

The other reason is that Kinetic made a strategic decision to use Nationwide's underwriting system regardless of whether they felt it was fit for purpose or what they would have liked to have. This was a very MVP-type decision, or 'Minimum Viable Product', which allowed them to move faster, though with compromises in functionality, usability, and efficiency. Kinetic has their own solution on the safety side and must manually re-key information between it and Nationwide's underwriting tools. While this isn't ideal for the long-term and something they're planning to solve for, it was good enough for a January 1st go-live and has allowed them to operate since then.

The first year being live wasn't the time for Kinetic to spend time or money on having all the ideal, final answers to things like what their system should or shouldn't be. Instead, it was the time to prove that there is a market for their unique insurance offering. As Elhawary said, "The risk right now is about whether the market wants it, and then we can invest in doing it more smoothly."

That echoes the main initial concern or hesitation Hoppe had. He said, "I wondered if the mainstream market was really ready for a wearable device. Would they wear and use it to the degree that the self-insured space did? Will they respond when it buzzed? But the story was compelling enough that it was worth going for."

I asked whether the venture team had to push anyone or add urgency to get Kinetic's needs prioritized and acted on faster. Anderson and Hoppe agreed that isn't how it happened or how they work more broadly, despite any money the company has invested. Anderson said, "Ventures will always listen to the business and tries to serve the startup and the business together. This is about collaboration, not stepping on people. That openness builds awareness across the organization of what they're trying to do, and to do it inclusively. That makes it easier to build senior level support when you do it the right way."

Kinetic shared a few things they learned in the process and that stood out about Nationwide specifically. Elhawary said he always felt like it was a collaboration rather than a subordinate relationship. He said that the Kinetic team, "didn't feel like we had to have an answer to every question Nationwide had tomorrow. They recognized that there are some unknowns here, and we need to spend some time in the market learning."

Despite the collaborative efforts to write a policy in January 2022, that's not when the first policy ended up being written by Kinetic. Instead, they bound their first risk in *December 2021*.

> "This is about collaboration, not stepping on people. That openness builds awareness across the organization of what they're trying to do, and to do it inclusively."
>
> – Brian Anderson
> Partner,
> Nationwide Ventures

This set Kinetic up to get to do the in-market learning Elhawary mentioned as being so important. They've found that the market is, in fact, ready for this kind of solution, and has responded very well. Adoption by insureds reached 75% as of the end of 2022, against a goal of half of all accounts deploying the technology.[1] This kind of adoption and engagement bodes well for Kinetic's future fundraising efforts to help the company to push ahead on its MGA plans even further.

Kinetic has also exceeded Nationwide's premium and loss performance expectations so far, though Elhaway shows he's learned a lot about insurance by cautioning that it's too early to claim loss ratio victory as the book still needs to develop. First year premium production was 12x what Nationwide had forecasted, and frequency is running 25% below industry standards for the classes, states, and payroll Kinetic covers.

They also found that their sense of needing to own their own distribution was the right decision. Many brokers are not sure about new solutions or changes to how they've always worked, which can make it hard to find success with them. However, there are cohorts of brokers who are open to innovative, new approaches like this, and they see it as a way to set themselves apart in the market and win business. You need to identify those brokers and get them into the fold. These innovative brokers take business from the more hesitant brokers, who then have come to Kinetic asking for access to their product so they can start selling it.

> "They recognized that there are some unknowns here, and we need to spend some time in the market learning."
>
> – Haytham Elhawary
> Co-Founder & CEO, Kinetic

But Elhaway shared that they have not yet taken enough business from the large, established brokers for them to come to Kinetic – though it's still early days, of course.

Currently, Kinetic underwrites accounts as if there is no adoption or benefit from Kinetic's solution, and they issue a dividend to insureds who adopt and benefit from it. This has allowed Kinetic to solve for regulatory filing constraints and the need for more historical data to be able to price the benefit in at inception rather than provide it later,

---

[1] This means 75% of insured companies have deployed Kinetic's solution to some extent rather than 75% of workers at all insureds using it. Given that not every employee would be at risk of the types of injuries Kinetic aims to prevent, such as many office workers, you would not expect to see every employee use or benefit from Kinetic's solution.

which they're working on. They're able to price first year experience in second year policies with a stronger weighting than is typical in the industry, which helps solve for this constraint on renewals.

Working on this takes collaboration and cooperation between Kinetic and Nationwide. What Kinetic has found on that front is that Nationwide has been exceptionally responsive and flexible, which is important as both companies are navigating through uncharted waters. One thing Kinetic found early on is that they were uncompetitive in some states due to Nationwide's filing. Nationwide took in that feedback (and the data around it) and has already filed updated rating plans in those states, allowing Kinetic to compete more effectively and help protect their renewals from churn.

Kinetic's MGA agreement with Nationwide also reflects this idea of simplicity up front with openness to adjustment. Nationwide offered Kinetic a more straight forward commission structure with a generous base commission, but less room for profit sharing. This de-risked Kinetic's revenue stream (which is beneficial for subsequent fundraising) and allowed for an easier negotiation because they did not have to engage on the unknown of profitability given how new Kinetic's solution was. While that made things easier up front, it also limited Kinetic's potential upside to benefit from the success of their solution. After a year of positive results, the two sides re-looked at the model, and agreed to a more at-risk split between base commission and profit commission.

Elhawary describes the relationship in this way, "We bring them a problem, and they just go and solve it. We've had very few instances where they say they can't solve it."

While the early MGA results are impressive and worth celebrating, perhaps most importantly, workers are not suffering injuries like before, thanks to Kinetic. Elhawary shared that an auto dealer they insured who did not opt to use the wearables had a back injury claim during the first week of coverage. It was something their solution would have caught in real time and could have helped avoid. After the injury, Kinetic took that opportunity to bring up the wearables again, knowing the insured would now understand first-hand why this is important and worth trying. They accepted the idea this time, and there has not been another injury since.

And to the original reason why Elhawary wanted to reduce workplace injuries at scale – his mother's own story – the first elder care facility they insured has had no losses in their first year with Kinetic. While that's only one year and only one data point, the profound message in it is not lost on Elhawary. He said, "During COVID, society started calling these workers 'essential' whereas most people didn't even seem to notice them before. Now, we see how important they are to our lives, and how they're impacted by injury."

Foundations for The Future

- When a solution is in its early days, both sides need to be open to what they will learn by trying and be willing to adjust.

- Innovation and venture teams are invaluable for carriers to see what is on the horizon, but many struggle to commercialize what they see because there is too strong a divide between these units and the business. Finding ways to connect innovation and investment arms and business units or functions is critical to ensure these efforts aren't lost and new solutions don't flounder or fizzle.

- Be open to learning from each other as each side has expertise and perspective the other can benefit from. Insurers can learn new, more flexible ways of addressing problems or seizing on opportunities while insurtechs can benefit from industry depth and insight.

- Don't try to over-complicate everything up front, including finding ways to work with standard contracts or break things down into phases to come back to after a period of time. For example, rather than trying to solve for every possibility or need up front, consider using a first-year agreement with room to adjust in the second year and beyond as you learn.

5. Mountain West Farm Bureau & Guidewire

Core system replacement projects are hard. Every carrier I have spoken to in my career says as much, as do I, having lived through three of them myself. The joke I often make is that you are in year five of your three-year core system project.

We all get it. These are massive undertakings, with lots of complications and dependencies, resource constraints and more. Too often, budgets overrun, timelines stretch and delivered scope pales in comparison to what was envisioned. If not very carefully governed and managed, in the end, despite all the promises made upfront, people often are not happy with what they have, which can unfortunately be a recreation of their old systems and processes, just less familiar looking.

In these situations, all of the odd ways we work get rebuilt into the new system despite being functions of past system constraints we faced when defining our processes. While we may have retired our legacy systems, the ghosts of them live on, haunting every effort to sunset those systems and the ways they hold our businesses back.

As an example, on my first core system project, of which I was the business lead, I remember an underwriter being shown the quoting workflow we had developed, and how he could generate a rate on a D&O policy in minutes rather than the hour-plus he needed in our legacy system. After getting a rate, he could just hit a button and send a quote to the broker.

Upon seeing this, the underwriter got very upset. The team and I were dumbfounded, as we expected him to love it.

Instead, he told us how he didn't want to send the quote himself, because then the brokers would come back to him with questions, changes, etc., whereas today, they ask his underwriting assistant for these things since that is who sends the quote out.

But not to worry, he had a solution! He said, "I don't want a button that sends the quote to the broker. I want a button that sends it to my UA and tells her to press another button to send it to the broker."

To be sure I hadn't misunderstood, I asked him to clarify that he wanted us to create a button he could press that told someone else to press another button that would then send the quote to the broker.

He eagerly confirmed this is what he wanted, seeming relieved that we understood what he needed.

One of the business analysts proposed a more efficient solution, asking if we could just let him press that one button, and have the quote go out from his UA's email address without creating another workflow item in the process. This seemed like a great if not obvious solution to the problem.

He got upset again. We were dumfounded again.

"No, because something will go wrong, and it will end up coming from me. You will say you didn't have time to build it that way or you'll mess it up somehow, and I'll get stuck with this, and then the brokers will be bothering me all day."

So, we built a button that tells someone to press another button to send a quote out (lowering our heads in shame in the process).

I wish I could say that was the only such story on that project, or on the projects I saw at other carriers over the years. And I wish I could say we all realize this is not ideal and are willing to change. I'd love it if we could stop working the same way so we can break the cycle and put in new core systems faster and with the freedom to let them work with the richness and efficiency with which they were designed.

The bad news is, I can't say that for the industry as a whole right now.

But it's not all negative. There is good news here, too. There's still hope that we *can* change, and the example of how Mountain West Farm Bureau stood up Guidewire InsuranceSuite on Guidewire Cloud in a year is perhaps the richest story I've come across in showing us all what's possible and how we can do better.

Mountain West, a Farm Bureau insurer headquartered in Laramie, Wyoming, writes roughly a quarter-billion-dollars in annual premium across personal lines (Auto, Home, Inland Marine, Liability, Umbrella, Farm & Ranch, and a country home product) and commercial (Auto,

BOP, and Commercial Package Policies) in Wyoming, and Montana, and in Colorado via their other writing company, 360 Insurance.

Like many carriers, they ran on mainframe-based systems for years, which they migrated to AS/400 servers, but they essentially worked the same as in their mainframe days. The company had worked to modernize its systems before, with three attempts ending fairly unsuccessfully, leaving them back where they started with five different core systems from a mix of vendors.

Two of their past efforts that failed involved Guidewire, with a deployment of an on-premises billing solution (Guidewire BillingCenter) being rolled back to their legacy system, and an attempt at an on-premises claims solution (Guidewire ClaimCenter) being abandoned before deployment in 2017. It's hard to say precisely why each of those attempts wasn't successful, but for a proven platform, it's rarely the technology itself, but rather details in how the project went.

Whether with Guidewire or others, each of these projects looked and felt like the situations I described above. Mountain West had spent a significant amount of money on each project and kept needing to spend a few million more and extend a few more years, ultimately not getting what they needed.

And like so many of these projects across the industry, an army of vendors and systems integrators (SIs) were involved, often running the show, and being squarely positioned in the place of blame. It's never us who failed, but vendors who keep taking longer, charging more, and failing to deliver.

After years of this pain, CEO Jim Geesey decided they needed to rethink their entire approach, and brought in a new CIO from outside the industry who had extensive experience with projects like this. He found Tim Hays, who had completed 30 enterprise resource planning (ERP) projects across the manufacturing, real estate, and distribution spaces over his career. ERPs are the closest thing outside of insurance to core system projects inside it, making his experience and track record highly attractive. Hays joined Mountain West and started the job on September 28th, 2020.

Hays came in with a very different mindset than was common in the industry, and different than the assumptions of his new team based on their experience of what was possible.

Hays said, "I've seen this work in other industries, and kept asking why it's so much harder and time consuming in insurance? How can insurance be so different from manufacturing?" This questioning why it had been harder in insurance and not accepting "because that's how we've always done it" answers he was getting would drive his approach and define that of Mountain West going forward.

Hays started by taking an inventory of all the systems and solutions Mountain West was running, and said, "I stopped counting at 150, which is an impossible mission for this size organization to manage effectively. Some of the systems were business critical, but the vendors behind them weren't even in business anymore. With that many disparate and potentially unsupported systems, you never knew what would break next, and every day, it seemed like something would."

Geesey had hired Hays to put in a new system, expecting it would be a five to seven-year transition, as was the norm in the industry, but as he took stock of the current situation, Hays quickly realized how much more urgent things were.

In early November, the two talked about potential approaches, with Geesey feeling strongly that Guidewire was the right solution provider to work with despite the unsuccessful attempts in the past. Mountain West had been talking to another Farm Bureau insurer who had a successful deployment of Guidewire up and running and the companies negotiated a potential solution to 'rent out' expanded usage of that deployment to Mountain West as an option to meet their needs.

Hays accepted that Guidewire was a good fit for their needs but wasn't settled on the proposed subletting-type approach as the right way to do it. He realized he didn't have enough information yet and worked to dig into what Guidewire was capable of and what options Mountain West had with them. He worked with Guidewire to learn about their entire offering, both on-prem and cloud, and even got to the level of understanding the licensure and accounting involved in both.

On December 1st, Hays presented his thoughts to Geesey and the rest of the leadership team and had a bold ask of them. After looking at their options, he wanted the team to look at Guidewire Cloud and asked to have a demo workshop before Christmas.

To his surprise, they all said yes.

Hays worked with a team including Guru Venkataramu and Joe Scinto, Guidewire's lead on the implementation and the customer success manager for Mountain West, respectively, to make the workshop happen on such short notice. Guidewire's approach would be to gather some general requirements and learn about how Mountain West worked to prepare a demo built for Mountain West's needs.

Hays wanted to take a different approach. Contrary to how most of these projects begin, he didn't want to start by bending Guidewire to what the business thought it needed. That would extend timelines, add cost, and increase complexity. Instead, he wanted the business to see what Guidewire can do out of the box, see if there were any deal breakers, and then decide the best way to work through them. Given the urgency and past experience, Hays saw the need to keep things as out of the box as possible, and that would be hard to do if they started the entire process with an eye to fitting Guidewire Cloud to how Mountain West had been working historically.

Guidewire understood the concerns and desired approach but was equally concerned that they would be showing the business something that – without the basics of familiar product definitions or Mountain West nomenclature – felt so foreign and ill-suited to their needs that it would be dismissed right off the bat. They settled on doing two demos, one out-of-the-box, and one focused around using the other Farm Bureau's system given Mountain West's current ways of working.

> "You must go in with the idea that the software will work."
>
> – Tim Hays
> VP & CIO,
> Mountain West
> Farm Bureau
> Insurance

Coming out of the workshops and demos with Guidewire, it was clear to both companies that a fresh start was the right path rather than Mountain West inheriting all the past decisions of the other Farm Bureau insurer. Even with the demo of InsuranceSuite on the cloud being a vanilla version with no special accommodations for how Mountain West said they needed to work, the team felt it was a better fit and decided to move ahead.

From making that decision just before the end of the year, Mountain West had signed a subscription agreement for InsuranceSuite on Guidewire Cloud on January 8th, 2021, an incredibly short time not just for a decision, but to decide and sign a commercial agreement for a major software implementation. This kind of speed became a hallmark of the project not by chance, but by intention.

Hays said that they could move this fast for a few reasons. Because he had done similar projects so many times before, he was familiar with many aspects of it, where the traps lay, and how to navigate them. But he also gave credit to the mindset Mountain West had, that the software would work, and work out of the box as a critical factor.

He said:

"You must go in with the idea that the software will work. If you're signing a contract and still questioning whether it will work, there are one of two problems. First, if you don't think it will work, you need to move on. Second, if you don't think it will work to your satisfaction, then it's probably because you don't think you can change your organization enough to work with it out of the box, and then you need to move on."

By engaging in the contract negotiations from that perspective, the tenor and approach changes from one where both sides assume everything would go wrong and needing to protect yourself from that to one where you're collaborating on the premise of it succeeding.

Guidewire specifically noted how Hays separated redlining the agreement from the business discussion around the content of it. That meant they weren't trying to understand each other while sending drafts with edits back and forth. Instead, they discussed the substance, and then redlined what needed to change in the contract given that conversation, knowing they were already on the same page.

Hays worked to thoroughly understand not just the terms of the agreement, but the functionality, approach and roadmap being agreed to. Both companies felt this was critical, not just to speeding up the contracting process, but to the success of the program because the key contact in the business understood the technical, legal, and business aspects involved so deeply.

Many companies will outsource contract negotiations to their legal team, vendor management function or outside counsel. While having that expertise involved is valuable, it does not absolve the business from taking the lead on the substance of the contract, which is exactly what Hay's involvement ensured in this case.

That's not to say Mountain West didn't have changes to the contract, or that it didn't take people on both sides working tirelessly to get it turned around quickly, but that effort would not have resulted in such a fast signing had Mountain West engaged in the process differently.

Not only did they sign the contract quickly, but Hays insisted they target completion of development of the project in a year. This would take not just changing how they do projects, but so much about how Mountain West works that the company would emerge with a new system and potentially new culture and operating philosophy on the other side. The leadership team, alongside Hays, understanding the importance of this venture, built the Guidewire effort into their overall strategic planning to further ensure its success.

Hays also worked to ready the organization for this effort in the areas of staffing and structure. He reorganized the internal IT department, established a project management intake and structure, and set expectations on a cadence that would be required in order to reach these goals. Internal and external teams were brought into the project together and vendor relationships were established to help fill talent gaps.

Mountain West's collective ownership of this project was paramount to its success. Hays knew it could not just be an IT project. He worked with leadership and each of the other departments to identify leads and subject matter experts who were given direction and empowered to make decisions.

Guidewire had rarely seen insurers push for and deliver to such aggressive timelines for this level of scope (and even less frequently succeed), which concerned them about achieving the target timeline. They were also mindful of patterns they saw when working with Mountain West in the past, where things played out more like they do in other notorious core system projects discussed at the start of this chapter. While they raised their concerns to Hays, they also recognized the people, technology, approach, and – most importantly – mindset were completely different, so they were up for the challenge. Like Hays believing the software would work, Guidewire believed Mountain West and Guidewire would work on the project together effectively and at a blistering pace.

One issue that came up as they went to sign would not impact contracting *per se* but would either mean a major customization would be needed or that Guidewire would not be a viable option for Mountain West unless the business was willing to make a material change.

Because Mountain West offered a package policy, as many Farm Bureau insurers do, they would need to be able to maintain that offering going forward. InsuranceSuite, however, does not have the concept of package policies. Instead, it has a similar yet different concept of rolling up individual policies to an account level that can then be billed together.

This was a major strategic decision and fork in the road for Mountain West. Getting InsuranceSuite to work this way would take major changes if it was even possible. Hays recognized this could be one of those factors that leads to project failure, as had happened with past failed core system projects. Yet not getting it to work this way would be a major shift in product and marketing strategy for Mountain West on something many of the Farm Bureaus see as a competitive advantage in the marketplace.

Decisions like this take time because they are big, but also because they need to rise up to a senior level across several functions, which may require the project to wait for steering committee meetings to occur, or a series of different meetings to take place and feed into each other. It would not be unreasonable to see this as a one-month or even one-quarter long decision at most carriers, if not longer.

Hays knew they didn't have that luxury, not just for this decision, but also for setting the tone of how they would make decisions, big and small, on this project. This is another area where Hays' insight proved to be on target. In establishing the project structure and cadence, Hays needed to make sure they did not get stuck waiting for decisions. He set weekly steering committee meetings with the understanding that everyone on it was empowered to make decisions on the spot, and that no part of the business was left out of the room. This meant Jim Geesey had to be at each of these meetings along with the rest of the executive team. This is the group Hays raised this issue to, and quickly got a decision that Mountain West would shift its approach to these package policies, allowing the project to move ahead.

Hays initially got pushback about the frequency of these meetings, but after seeing how they were able to navigate big decisions like this and keep the project on target, group sentiment shifted.

Resourcing is also a common source of delays, whether in a steering committee, requirements gathering, testing or other part of big projects like this. Hays said:

"You must have people on the project who can make a decision, and you can't outsource that to consultants who can't make decisions about *your* business every day. They don't have to live with it. All they can do is recommend. If the people you put on your project aren't painful to take out of your business, you picked the wrong people."

Too often, Hays had seen companies employ SIs and then blame them or system vendors for problems. That's not to say you shouldn't use SIs or buy from vendors – both things that happened on this project – but doing so doesn't change who is responsible for what happens, and therefore every business leader needs to be engaged and own the outcome.

Hays said, "Asking if the vendor will keep you on track is the wrong question. It's *your* project. If it succeeds or fails, it's *your* success or failure. You wrote the check; you made the decisions."

With the package policy roadblock removed and the contract signed, something Geesey said to Guidewire early on was put into action. He said, "I want to cross the starting line running. That isn't the time we start the race."

The starting line was set as March 26th, 2021.

From signing the contract in January, both companies had work to do to ensure they were at full speed as they crossed that line. For Mountain West, that meant training the team on Guidewire's product, but also on its approach to development, called SurePath. Agile development was still new to Mountain West, so Guidewire's tried-and-true approach to and training for it was invaluable. For Guidewire, they used the time to provision their product for Mountain West, get to build relationships with the carrier's people, and do extensive planning for the project.

They would divide the year into 13 20-day sprints, which Hays said were long enough to do meaningful work they could demonstrate, test and deploy, which shorter sprints wouldn't allow. This was also not so long that people lost the plot between releases (as can be common with

> "Asking if the vendor will keep you on track is the wrong question. It's your project. If it succeeds or fails, it's your success or failure."
>
> – Tim Hays
> VP & CIO, Mountain West Farm Bureau Insurance

Waterfall methodology) or that development had gotten too off track before having the chance to course correct if needed.

They began on March 26th with a virtual meeting for everyone involved. Guidewire CEO Mike Rosenbaum joined the call, which surprised the Mountain West team. Hays had been connecting Geesey and Rosenbaum ahead of this meeting, so the two CEOs knew each other and were aligned. As Hays said, "You don't want the first time they talk to be when there's a problem." This sent a message to the Mountain West team that, just as Hays talked about holding themselves responsible for every decision, Guidewire was holding itself responsible, right up to the top. This helped instill confidence in the project for the team.

> "I want to cross the starting line running. That isn't the time we start the race."
>
> – Jim Geesey
> President & CEO,
> Mountain West Farm Bureau Insurance

Confidence was a recurring theme throughout the project. Guidewire and Hays noticed how the Mountain West team almost had a crisis of confidence from their past experiences. Hays talked about the skepticism and cynicism that resulted at Mountain West (and the industry) around believing any timeline or functionality promised to them from new systems. This sentiment is understandable, and one both Guidewire and Hays set out to change at Mountain West, starting with that kickoff meeting.

After Guidewire had outlined the solution and approach, Hays stood up and announced that InsuranceSuite on Guidewire Cloud works right out of the box. He went further – at the risk of getting blow back from the room – by saying, "I don't care what you don't like about this software or what you'd do differently. That's not your job. Your job is to tell me why it won't work, not what you don't like. We need to keep this out of the box. I presume 85% of what it can do will work for us as is."

To his surprise, he did not get any push back to his bold words, though he soon realized why. It wasn't that people agreed with him, it's that they were just so numb to statements like this that they presumed it was wrong. They expected that the project would go on for some time, fail, and then would be replaced by another project, so they just had to live through this process.

Essentially, they ignored him.

Skepticism aside, the project started in earnest. As sprints were completed, functionality was demoed to the business, with Hays insisting that only Mountain West people do the demos and work on anything that needed adjusting coming out of them. This was critical for him and something Guidewire felt contributed to the building of confidence in Mountain West's culture.

This ensured Mountain West's people knew the system intimately and understood how the business saw it. It also increased their sense of ownership of every feature and delivery because they were the ones on the frontlines, demonstrating functionality to their peers. In this way, they got immediate, direct feedback on how something was received, whether good or bad. It also built a sense of collaboration between IT and the people in other departments. Their familiarity with the people doing the demo also helped the business feel more connected to what they were seeing, increasing their buy-in to the new system.

While things were going well, there were also problems brewing. With COVID still impacting how people worked, development resources were scattered across a dozen or more time zones, people were getting sick or facing certain restrictions periodically, and more. Adding the normal impact of people taking vacation time, scope creeping or proving bigger than initially estimated, and inevitable instances of delivery not being smooth and linear, the project started to see slippage as some development already began to get pushed out by the June sprint.

With Mountain West needing to start retiring their legacy systems in January, slippage would be hard to accommodate by merely moving the dates out, as many projects do. This is also how the inevitable "a few more years and a few more million dollars," pattern Hays had warned about begins.

The team looked at the solutions immediately available to it and did what they could. Hays said, "The way to get fast is to stop being slow," meaning you look at why you're going the pace you are, identify the causes, and ask what would happen if you removed some or all of them. They trimmed scope that could be trimmed. They looked at ways to get more efficient in their work and implemented them.

Being a project management purist, Hays pushed his team to report progress on a daily basis. Some pushed back, saying this was an inefficient use of their time. Instead of taking time while working on something to report their progress, they would just mark it done when they completed it. For Hays, that meant he would be in the dark about how it was going, with work showing 0% complete and then suddenly being 100% done. He insisted on daily reporting despite the push back, saying, "It's a day's work in a day, not a sprint's work in a sprint." If he saw work that was 20% done when 60% of the time had elapsed, he could try to help solve for why that is – the developer could be overloaded or could be working inefficiently. Either case requires intervention. But there's nothing he could do about what he didn't know.

Hays talked about this with the team as being fanatical about execution, and using data as sunlight, acting like a disinfectant for problems.

Despite these efforts, by August, it was clear that there simply wasn't enough capacity on the team at Mountain West or Guidewire and its partners to defend the timeline. After knowing they had exhausted every available option, Hays turned to Guidewire leadership to help find another solution. They were able to identify additional resources from Guidewire's partners that could be added to the project to get it back on target.

While this may sound like the end of the story on this potential threat to the project, anyone who has been in such situations knows even resolving it doesn't resolve it. There can be lasting distrust, animosity or adversariness to the working relationship. But because of the way the engagement began, with deep understanding on both sides, Mountain West owning the ultimate success and failure, and the openness with which both companies had been working together on this problem, the resolution of it felt mutual and complete.

When observing similar situations in the past, I've found that there is often hiding of the truth about slippage, finger pointing as to the cause, arguments over who is responsible for solving or paying for it, and more. Here, the problem was visible to everyone, there was a constant and collaborative engagement on trying to solve it with what was in front of them, and then a united approach to looking beyond that for a bigger solution.

This collaborative approach between Guidewire and Mountain West was echoed internally between IT and the business and was equally critical in the project's success. Not only were the best people from the business needed throughout the project, but Mountain West would also not be able to go live with a successful system if it wasn't embraced by the business users. Between their past bad experiences with system projects and the hard line drawn around using the system as it was out of the box, there was a strong risk that the business users would not be happy with what they were given.

It wasn't as simple as just being unhappy as all the leaders in the business were also sign off authorities for the system, meaning Hays could not claim victory without their support.

As development went on, the frequent demonstrations of what was being built and the way feedback was taken in helped to warm and even excite the business to what was coming at the end of the project. The engagement of key businesspeople throughout the project also helped build a coalition of supporters from around the company.

But one major hurdle remained – Mountain West's agents. That's not to say the agents were blocking the project, but agents had been on the receiving end of the past system failures, and the company felt they could not risk disappointing their agents again.

Mountain West addressed this in two ways. First, they brought in a select group of agents during the project to get an early look at the system, what it would enable for Mountain West (and, in turn, for what they could do for agents and insureds) and solicited feedback and guidance from those agents.

Second, Mountain West took a long and deliberate path in their user acceptance testing (UAT) after the system was done. With the resources added in August 2021, the project ended up hitting its 12-month delivery date, nearly to the day, with completion of the technical requirements on March 21, 2022. However, the system wouldn't truly go live in the market for another four months, after a pilot in Colorado in May with 360 Insurance. That time was dedicated to ensuring everything worked as needed and Mountain West's staff and agents were trained and ready to work in the new system.

This isn't an unusual approach, but it was a marked slowdown from the path up to this point, and it was deliberate. There were specific criteria for each member of the executive team to say the system was ready, including that there were no outstanding issues, no outstanding critical functionality, staff had been successfully trained, agents were properly educated and engaged, etc. The project team created a signoff game to get people excited about it and build some healthy internal competition, making Sign Off Bingo cards.

When a functional lead raised a reason not to sign off, the team engaged in the specifics behind the decision so they could address it. If someone pushed back on a lack of functionality, it was quickly prioritized into a sprint so people could see that their need was being met and could sign off. If training wasn't sufficient, a training plan was further developed or adapted and deployed to show how the gap was to be closed.

Hays said that this was the one place where he slowed down and stopped pushing hard. He also said he gave grace here that he wouldn't give again in the future because the people giving signoff had been disappointed so much before that he couldn't expect them to simply have faith and trust that all would work out without being able to see it clearly.

He elaborated he wouldn't *have* to give them that grace again because the business has learned from this experience. The functions saw that the project delivered on its word, and issues were resolved openly and collaboratively. And with the sunlight of data, they could watch gaps being closed in real-time.

In July 2022, Mountain West went live with their five lines of personal insurance in all states they write in. The proof was in the pudding. The team recorded only 23 level two or higher-severity issues in the first 90 days, and under 200 mostly non-critical issues by the end of 2022 against over 4,500 development items. And, proving this was more than just an internal success, feedback from agents and customers echoed these extremely positive technical results.

Hays shared that, as they prepared for the extension of the system to the final part of the business in 2023, he's found that he couldn't give the business the same grace, even if he wanted to. Instead, with this deployment, they asked how they could go faster rather than questioning whether they would ever get what they want. The business has made it clear that they want to get off the legacy systems and believe in what they're getting and when they're getting it.

The next delivery was three commercial lines of business, delivered in February 2023, and the full project is on target to be completed by the end of 2024.

Another key part of the program was data migration, which is a rare point where Hays said he made the wrong decision. This is where so many projects flounder, either struggling to do it at all, getting an incomplete migration, living with data errors and issues, or being stuck between systems far longer than expected. Hays sees this as a main reason traditional system projects suffer due to how long carriers end up with data caught between systems and no good way to bring it back together so they can run their business.

Guidewire had advocated for creating an automated approach to migration because of success they've had doing so with many of their other customers. Mountain West decided to migrate policies on renewal, which is the path many carriers take, as doing a mid-term migration can trigger regulatory issues if the products or rating don't completely align (which they often don't as rating engines are changed, and products are enhanced or refiled as part of many new system projects). It can also lead to customer friction and disruption due to data issues, which can ultimately negatively impact retention. Both key migration decisions, to automate it and migrate on renewal, were based on past success and best practices, so they moved ahead with the plan.

The team spent six months trying to create an automated data migration approach yet could not get it to work reliably. This could have been a function of the number of systems they were migrating from, the change in product structure for their package offering, something else, or a mix of factors. In some situations, like Mountain West found for themselves, automation can prove tricky – something I've seen at two carriers myself despite also seeing it go smoothly at others. As the first renewals approached, Hays made the call to revert to a manual data conversion effort as he felt they would end up in the same place either way, but were burning time and resource trying to automate, and it was time to cut their losses.

In hindsight, he said he would have made that decision from the start and save the six months of fruitless effort. He was concerned upfront that automating would be too complicated and risky and the effort to figure it out would be non-trivial. Because it isn't something they would need to do on an ongoing basis, it would have been better to just do it manually from the start. This perspective may change in the future, but in this situation, it was a cost to the project Hays regrets incurring.

On the back of this admission, I asked Hays whether the near dogmatic insistence on using InsuranceSuite as it was out of the box had been the right call, and if his sense that 85% of what the business needed would be met by the system without changing was accurate.

He said it wasn't accurate. Instead, they found that more like 90-95% of the functionality fit now that they're live, and that, sometimes, you don't know you could live with something the way it is until you actually try to because it looks so different from what you have that you can't possibly imagine it working. He asked the business to live with everything that wasn't a true showstopper before saying they had to create a custom solution and, invariably, that meant the request for a change was usually abandoned after the business had some time to adjust.

I liken this to the first time you take a shortcut on a familiar route you travel. Regardless of what the clock says, you usually feel like it took longer when using a new shortcut because of how different it feels. Once you acclimate, you recognize that it was better all along.

Guidewire added how much this contributed to Mountain West's success with the development and implementation phases of the project, but it doesn't stop there. Because they are using the system so close to how it was originally built, Mountain West has seen additional benefits.

First, they are positioned to take updates and new features quickly because there is little to no custom code to unwind or test against. Because of that, the carrier was the one of the first in-production Guidewire Cloud customers to upgrade to the latest version as of this writing (Guidewire's Flaine release). It also means Mountain West has access to a huge library of partner solutions deployed in Guidewire's Marketplace where other vendors make their solutions available via pre-built and tested APIs that can be enabled within your Guidewire Cloud environment.

To take advantage of this, Mountain West made a decision to always prioritize a vendor with a solution in the Marketplace when they had a choice between one in and out of the Marketplace. That might mean changing vendors for a given solution, but it creates flexibility and simplicity, while also giving Mountain West additional clout with that vendor by having Guidewire's scale added to their own needs from the vendor. As a smaller carrier, this can pay dividends down the road.

All of this speaks to a warning Hays made early on to the team at Mountain West. When thinking about customizing versus taking what's available out of the box, he cautioned that you don't just pay for customizations once. You pay for them every time you have to upgrade because of the complications they add to the upgrade or how they lead you to skip upgrades and increase your technical debt; you pay for them in the options you can't take advantage of or can't get to work, like all of the great Marketplace partners available to them; etc. Customizations may seem great in the moment, but they become a short-term benefit with exponentially greater long-term costs.

While this has worked out well for Mountain West, Guidewire does caution that the size of the project, complexity, and cost of a solution like this isn't necessarily a fit for every carrier. If Mountain West merely wanted to replace its legacy systems and operate as-is, InsuranceSuite would likely have been overkill on all fronts.

But Mountain West wasn't interested in "as-is". They were working to evolve and grow. While they did want and need to get off their legacy systems, this was more about being *free* of them. The company saw future potential in a mandate to operate differently, making InsuranceSuite ideal for them despite it being a big investment for their size. This enables Mountain West to have the advanced capabilities of a significantly bigger carrier, giving them the ability to punch above their weight.

And because Mountain West implemented in such an out of the box fashion, they've ensured they can deploy new capabilities and take advantage of them quickly. They have been part of Guidewire's Early Access program to get access to features before they're released and give feedback to Guidewire about the final version that gets built into new releases of Guidewire Cloud, like Flaine.

Mountain West could have chosen a smaller system with fewer features and less scalability that's more aligned to their current reality. But given the company's strategic plan, it would find the upfront savings of that approach to be a false economy that either constrained the company or lead them to have to do it all over again. And because Hays got so deep on the functionality and details of the licensing structure, Mountain West was able to start with capabilities that better match their current needs and budget without closing the door to the growth and capabilities they need as they grow.

With Hays being fanatical about execution, his focus on making decisions quickly, his insistence on not changing the system and more, you could think the lessons in this story is just about strict project management and adherence to Agile methodology.

For Guidewire, they see something much deeper than this, hitting at how Mountain West has emerged from the project. They went in with the scars of past projects and their impact on trust, courage, and collaboration. How they work now is materially different, and it is impossible not to notice. Guidewire's Chief Customer Officer, Christina Colby, said, "The past failures weighed heavy on the program. Mountain West realized they had to change to be able to do this. What was going to happen and what did ultimately happen, is that the success changed them."

Foundations for The Future

- Avoid your desire to work the way you've been working when implementing something new. See what it can do in totality first, assume that approach will work for you, and don't change anything unless there is literally no way for the business to operate if you don't.

- Contract negotiation is two different things that should be done separately – business dialog and redlining. Start by understanding the details and intention of every part of the contract, and then revise with a unified sense that the solution will do what it is supposed to do.

- Ensuring everyone is trained and aligned so you can speak the same language before the kickoff will allow you to begin the race before you hit the starting line.

- Making decisions quickly is critical to a project's success, and requires frequent, regular engagement of people empowered to make those decisions and who will be responsible for the implications of them. This cannot be outsourced any more than the day to day running of your business can.

- The weight of past failures is real and can continue to impact future efforts. Take deliberate actions to demonstrate that you do what you say, be open about where things stand and give those who mistrust a voice you are willing to hear but hold them to their part in solving problems.

6. Ohio Mutual & Pinpoint Predictive

Artificial Intelligence (AI) has been a buzzword the insurance industry has been talking about for years. Unlike other buzzwords like blockchain, AI has seen numerous actual applications, with adoption increasing in both use cases and carriers.

On the simpler end of the spectrum, insurers use AI to feed into basic decisions and actions in moments within a customer journey, like recognizing a question a customer is asking via text, and presenting basic information in response (e.g., "What's my claim rep's name?" And responding, "Your claim is being handled by Sally Jackson.")

On the more complex end, entire processes and workflows are being handled through AI, like automatically adjusting an Auto Physical Damage claim by analyzing the photos submitted by an insured and responding with a dollar value settlement the insured can accept, get paid electronically, and have their claim closed, all within minutes of an accident.

We also see AI being used more and more in underwriting situations, which invariably raises a common apprehension around explainability and transparency. Many insurers are concerned that regulators will require proof that rates are being determined fairly and consistently, which may be hard to do if an AI is setting them through some 'black box' mechanism that carriers cannot really pick apart and explain. It's an understandable concern, and one some solution providers are trying to solve in how their AI tools work.

The alternative, which so many carriers rely on in several lines of business, is credit score. Credit has proven to be the strongest single predictor of loss frequency and severity of anything the industry has ever used, explaining its wide adoption and continued usage across lines of business and carriers in the industry. At the same time, few things (if any) that are openly known to be inherently biased have continued to be used this widely. Credit scores have been demonstrated to be biased against different racial, ethnic, and socio-economic groups, while also being demonstrably uncorrelated to major drivers of loss ratios, like litigation propensity.

Despite its flaws, credit is something many insurers and most regulators are used to and understand, meaning we don't have to explain how it works in determining rate. Feeding a customer's name and address into an AI algorithm to get a price back does not have this level of comfort working in its favor. Even if it were to solve for the known issues with credit, we may not be able to clearly show how it worked, leaving it hard for regulators to accept.

This argument continues to keep many carriers on the sidelines of AI while some others have taken steps to understand and deploy it where they can. Eventually, solution providers will solve this issue, and those who have been engaging in AI deployment will be much farther along than their peers who only just start their journeys then, giving those earlier-adopters a clear leg up.

This dilemma is something Ohio Mutual Insurance Group (OMIG) was keenly aware of. As a smaller, regional player with deep community roots, they weren't ready to go full-bore on AI, but also recognized they needed to find ways to build comfort and expertise at a pace they, their agents and customers could all embrace.

The company has been on a path of embracing new ideas since CEO Mark Russell joined in the mid-2010s. I wrote about OMIG's journey of innovation in the first volume in this series, through the lens of their work with Hi Marley, an insurtech focused on fixing the communication struggles within claims. Something Russell did to help at that time was appoint an Actuary in the Business Analytics department, Ryan Ward, to lead a cross-functional group that was tasked with looking at different insurtech trends and solutions, tracking their trajectory and promise, and helping to bring those that seemed to be a fit for OMIG's needs into the business.

In that capacity, I reached out to Ward in August of 2020 with something I had come across that I thought OMIG might be curious about. It was a company called Pinpoint Predictive, and I learned about it while sitting on a panel with their founder and CIO, Avi Tuschman, at the last event I attended before lockdowns hit. Tuschman talked about using people's broader behavioral footprints to form predictive pictures of their propensities and proclivities that could be married with a carrier's data to predict different behaviors or actions people might take. What they built is a novel approach to using deep-learning algorithms to predict key behavioral risks in P&C insurance. It was something I had never seen before in how it took carrier data, enriched it, and made predictions about people's likelihood to behave in certain ways that could be applied before they even become an insured.

It was fascinating to me, and the accuracy of their predictions, which they could make on all adults in the U.S., left me thinking about all the possibilities for how this could help insurers make better, less biased decisions.

As a Claims professional, I could see it helping to predict someone's likelihood of seeking representation from an attorney or accepting a settlement offer, which could be valuable when quoting a new prospect. Tuschman talked about the benefits in risk selection or even earlier, when targeting your marketing efforts by predicting someone's likelihood to commit fraud, file a non-CAT claim, and more. As he and I talked about their solution in these early days, potential use cases grew. Since then, Pinpoint has developed specialization around predicting drivers of profitability earlier and more accurately than was possible before. To help them build to that vision, I was excited to share it with some carriers I had grown close to over the years, like OMIG, and see where the most value for insurers could be.

I wasn't exactly sure what the best use case would be for Ohio Mutual, but also knew them well enough to know they would have an open mind to see if there were ways this might be of value to their business. And if there weren't, they would still value looking at something different and challenging themselves to reflect on their business and ways to improve or seize on new opportunities.

We set up a meeting so the OMIG team could learn more about Pinpoint, see its solution in action, and talk about whether they saw potential for it.

It was a good and interesting discussion, but it was also clear that neither side knew what use case would make the most sense. For Pinpoint, it was still early in their journey in Insurance, so they had not yet built a library of "best practice" predictive models to readily match to Ohio Mutual's situation and needs, which they have subsequently done.

For OMIG, they hadn't been thinking about using a solution like this, so they had no apparent problem they were trying to solve. It was the proverbial 'technology in search of a solution' situation, and, as a result, while both parties were interested in *something*, neither knew what that might be, and things languished.

Part of the complication was that OMIG had not done anything material with AI before, so they were too new to it to find the right application for it immediately. They were also still a bit apprehensive around how to bring it safely and transparently into their business.

In the background was a problem many carriers with a Northern U.S. exposure base face. According to the National Fire Protection Association (NFPA), every year, over 46,000 homes burn from a fire started inside the home, and roughly 14% of those are started by home heating equipment. The main cause of these fires is solid fuel heating equipment, like wood-burning stoves (this can also include coal, wood-pellet and other, similar solid fuels).[2]

These fires don't just cause property loss, but also are the cause of a disproportionate number of fire deaths, at 19% of total deaths, according to NFPA. Clearly, the death and destruction are tragic, but it's even worse when you realize that a quarter of these fires are the result of the buildup of soot called creosote that happens when people don't properly maintain their equipment and chimneys. In other words, many of these events could likely have been prevented.[3]

For years, OMIG had done what most carriers do about this, asking questions about wood-burning stoves when writing new business, and including a question about them if they were to send a renewal questionnaire. On average, 5-6% of people have such stoves in their homes in OMIG's footprint, and roughly that proportion of people responded that they did have one when asked.

However, inevitably, some people will neglect to answer affirmatively if they do have a stove, perhaps because of a communication breakdown between the prospect and the agent, someone overlooking the question or possibly even someone not wanting to admit to having a stove. As some of these are homemade,

---

[2] Campbell, Richard, "Home Heating Fires," National Fire Protection Association, January 2021.
[3] Campbell, 2021.

the prospective customer may not want to disclose it for fear of getting a quote they cannot afford.

Something else OMIG learned is that word choice matters. If they referred to these stoves as "wood-burning stoves" and people had wood pellet, coal or other solid fuel stoves, they may say they didn't have one, which wouldn't be lying so much as making a very technical interpretation of the question. And, lastly, some people may not have had a stove at the time of buying their policy but got one after that and did not realize they needed to report this to their insurer.

Whether intentional or accidental, the result is that Ohio Mutual and other carriers are insuring a greater risk for homes with these stoves, yet they are carrying this increased exposure without the additional premium they should be charging for them. One way they learn about this is when one of those homes suffers a fire caused by the stove, which happens, leaving a carrier to either cover a loss they may not have properly priced for or deny coverage and face the fallout or legal battle that may result.

This is a perennial problem that gets attention in the winter months because that's when these fires usually occur. Carriers talk about how to solve for it, struggle to make progress, and then move on to other priorities as temperatures rise. Ohio Mutual is no different in this regard.

Along the way, they decided to see if there might be a better solution than asking insureds repeatedly and hoping for the best. With advances in aerial imagery, they wondered if this might present a solution as wood-burning stoves often have different chimneys than standard fireplaces.

In piloting a solution, OMIG learned a few issues with the approach. First, national imagery coverage percentages do not necessarily translate to strong coverage in OMIG's more rural footprint. This is similar to how cell phone coverage claims play out, with mobile phone providers claiming to cover 90-something percent of the country, but they mean that as a measure of population rather than geography. OMIG had trouble getting complete coverage of the homes they insure for this reason.

Second, these solutions are focused on things like signs of damage to or weakness in a roof, threats from vegetation overhang, etc. They aren't quite up to the level of being able to parse out the specifics of different cylindrical objects protruding from roofs or being able to see through vegetation to spot the chimneys, making them less ideal for this application.

Ohio Mutual had raised this wood stove issue as one of the potential things that might be of value to investigate with Pinpoint, but it was such an outsider case from what Pinpoint had worked on and didn't sound like the kind of thing either side thought would be a clear fit.

As their discussions started to lose energy, the 2020-2021 winter began, and OMIG faced a reminder of the wood-burning stove problem and thought this would at least be worth testing with Pinpoint.

Pinpoint saw this as a path of reducing premium leakage and avoiding losses, so even a couple of fires prevented would create material value for Ohio Mutual, and more than pay for the solution. OMIG, however, felt that the only way to avoid losses was to non-renew a risk they had written, and instead saw this as a risk prevention story through engagement with their agents and insureds, turning worse risks into better risks.

Vice President of Personal Lines, Chad Combs, whose business is where this idea would find an application, said of this mindset:

> "We are committed to trying to do something different at OMIG and change the value proposition insurance provides. We want to position Ohio Mutual to not just protect customers by fixing things after they happen, but to stop them from happening in the first place. That takes doing things differently, embracing insurtech and being open to change."

The two companies decided to test it out, working together to define what they needed to look at and how to do it over the summer of 2021. Ohio Mutual had a subset of insured homeowners that self-identified as having wood-burning stoves (that is, people checked the box in their new business application, or told OMIG when filling out a renewal questionnaire). OMIG would provide sample data to Pinpoint to see if their model could pick out these individuals as a way to see if its model accurately judged the likelihood that someone owned a wood-burning stove. This would help prove the accuracy and potential value of the solution to OMIG.

Aside from providing the data for Pinpoint to train its model on, this would take getting contracts in place. While a non-disclosure agreement (NDA) would be needed, it wouldn't be sufficient for the level of protection needed for the policyholder data involved. Many insurtechs use pilot agreements and statements of work (SOW) at this stage, negotiating terms and language with carriers to be sure both sides are protected. For OMIG, while that may give sufficient protection, it can also be a cumbersome process that ends up being a total waste if you find that the solution does not provide enough value. Having dealt with the specific issue they face with their more rural book, as was the case with aerial imagery coverage, they were especially concerned with expending effort on something that ends up not applying to their business.

To solve for that and allow them a nimbler way to test things while ensuring proper legal protection, they devised something they call their "NDA+", which takes the concept of an NDA, and extends it to account for the sharing of a sample of policyholder data for the purpose of a proof of concept. They standardized this document to apply to a broad set of use cases, allowing OMIG to put it in place quickly and consistently across solutions they evaluate.

This was developed as part of setting up their Procurement function, which has an eye to simplifying and standardizing contracts and working with a panel of outside counsel with different, specific areas of expertise so they have the right skillset for each opportunity. OMIG also spends time bringing these attorneys into the fold, so they understand the solution, what the pilot is aiming to achieve, the anticipated impact to the business, etc.

Having worked with more generalist counsel that isn't brought into the loop on what the solution aims to achieve before, I know this can slow things down dramatically as attorneys need to be able to understand the solution, its mechanics, and the implications for the contract. And if their background doesn't align with the type of solution being investigated, it can be hard for any attorney to be as efficient and effective as they could be with more thematic expertise.

Combs sees their investment in how they do procurement as critical to their ability to find the right answers and move on them fast. He said, "The quicker you can get to seeing what's redeeming about a solution, the better, so anything that delays it has this compounding effect. Sometimes, you're surprised by the outcome – in either direction – so you have to get it into practice as quickly as possible to figure it out."

Ward said that this was precisely the issue with Pinpoint. They weren't sure there was enough value in the approach, so a more involved process to get a sense of the value would have just led OMIG to pass on the opportunity. He said, "The hurdle would have been too much to bother with it. Streamlining allowed us to give things a try at lower internal cost and time, so we can see what's actually worth pursuing."

Between this strategy on the contracts and the way OMIG engages outside counsel, neither company found the contracting to stand in the way, as can often be the case, signing an agreement in September, and having results in October.

> "The quicker you can get to seeing what's redeeming about a solution, the better, so anything that delays it has this compounding effect."
>
> – Chad Combs
> VP, Personal Lines, Ohio Mutual

At over a year from the initial conversations, this is quite a long time, but most of it was spent with the two companies looking for a good fit and would have gone faster if they had a particular problem to solve up front. Pinpoint primarily provides loss predictions, but through the collaboration with OMIG felt confident the platform could solve other, more niche problems. Once the problem was identified, the process went quickly, with Pinpoint able to return results to OMIG within only a day.

The initial findings were quite strong. OMIG had set a success criteria for the test around the level of accurately predicting likelihood of wood-burning stove ownership (or not), and found the results surpassed that mark. This paved the way for the two companies to move to the next stage.

Pinpoint's model creates percentile buckets of customers based on behavior patterns and predicts their likelihood of owning a stove. The spread from the top to bottom decile (the 10% of homes most likely to the 10% least likely to own a wood-burning stove) was 20x, meaning knowing someone is in the top decile rather than the bottom suggests they're 20 times more likely to own a stove, and therefore you should inquire further if they say they don't. The Pinpoint team did some further refining of their model, increasing the spread to 30x, making it even more powerful in its ability to spot someone who likely has a stove regardless of what they reported.

Ohio Mutual was impressed by what they saw, but still had questions about what to do about it. Pinpoint provides continuous probabilities for the attributes of interest (percent-likelihood of having a wood-burning stove), so the results can be used on their own as an immediately deployable end prediction in accordance with the carrier's risk appetite. This makes the results clearly and immediately actionable. But the questions were what action to take, how do you take them, and how would the economics play out?

Underlying these questions were other points of uncertainty. For example, Pinpoint could accurately predict ownership in a dataset OMIG knew had stoves. Would it still predict it as well in the population more broadly? Could it be that there are so few unreported stoves that they would simply exist in the margin of error in a full deployment?

How would using these predictions look in OMIG's business? If they saw that someone likely had a stove, what would they have to do to verify ownership; find out the details about it like brand; who installed it; maintenance of it; etc.? What would such an effort cost?

Would engaging with customers about it result in them properly maintaining their equipment or removing it if it was too hazardous (like a homemade stove located in a dangerous area)? Would customers simply move to another insurer because of this effort?

Would agents be upset with the effort, fight against it, and start placing business with competitors?

Would the reduced premium leakage and contained fire exposure offset the costs involved?

Finally, would this be the right way to test the AI waters for OMIG, teaching them enough yet not crossing over into something they can't explain or be comfortable with?

These were very real questions OMIG would have to work through in deciding if and how to proceed. They started by recognizing there was no way to answer the first question about whether Pinpoint's model would work when applied to the entire book or not, so in January 2022, they decided to take a leap of faith and trust that the test findings would hold up. Or, because the findings were so strong, even if they didn't hold up completely, they would hold up enough to be worth it still.

Second, they had to design a process that would respect where they were on their AI journey, how they wanted customers and agents to feel, and give OMIG confidence they were operating in accordance with their values. Pinpoint met this need through the suite of explainable data visualization tools OMIG had access to rather than acting as an unexplainable 'black box'. As Combs described it, "We needed a safe way to start in on AI. We need to make sure we got the decision right and to be careful, but we also don't want to keep our eyes closed, either."

That led to a few key decisions.

Christina Roderick, on the Personal Lines Underwriting team, took the lead on these next steps. First, they wanted to do this only on renewals as they did not want to disrupt their new business process or their agents. They had existing solutions for doing renewal questionnaires, so there was a ready-made process they could add this into that agents were comfortable with and OMIG had already built, so this could be easily deployed.

They work with a third-party company who surveys customers pre-renewal, with defined follow up and escalation protocols between the vendor and OMIG. The vendor would send a survey in the mail and would follow up with a second mailing if they received no response. If there was still no response, they would then call the insured. If there was no response at that point, OMIG decided not to press the matter since, today, they didn't know whether the insured had a wood-burning stove or not, so OMIG was no worse off than before.

If the vendor got a positive response, they would alert Ohio Mutual, and would then send a follow up survey asking for details about the stove. If there was no response to *this* survey, Ohio Mutual would take over, working with the agent as they now knew there was a wood-burning stove that had not been previously reported to them, and had to get clarity on the situation or potentially mark the account for non-renewal.

This meant that OMIG was double confirming the existence of the stove after Pinpoint predicted that one exists that had not been disclosed. This came first through the initial survey, and then with the follow up questionnaire on the details about it. Those two things happened before OMIG took any action on the account, whether on rate or insurability. This satisfied Combs' need for safety and certainty in their decision and acting in accordance with Ohio Mutual's values.

Agent perception of the efforts was also crucial to OMIG's decision making, which is not surprising given their internal focus on agent satisfaction, measured by NPS (as discussed in the first volume of this series). To this end, they trained all their underwriters and sales staff on what they were doing so agents would be able to get their questions answered no matter who they spoke to at OMIG.

Knowing their agents, OMIG knew that a loss prevention approach would appeal to them since agents don't want insureds facing fire loss either, and recognize that this is a real issue. Adding that there was no disruption to agent workflows, no additional ask of agents, and that agents would be informed of who was being surveyed, what the response was, and what action OMIG was taking as a result, they saw little risk to their agent relationships.

While defining the plan of action, OMIG and Pinpoint worked on a commercial contract for this deployment. This is often an area of complication for OMIG given their scale relative to larger carriers. Being smaller means OMIG's budgets are smaller, and that large implementation fees become untenable relative to the potential value of a new solution. And with all the unknowns they faced, OMIG wasn't sure what the value would be once they went live, leaving them apprehensive of a fixed-price, front-loaded deal. The team at Pinpoint was aware of this concern on OMIG's part – and for smaller carriers more broadly – and used that sensitivity in how they framed their proposal.

With this in mind, Pinpoint proposed a fixed-price approach that was scaled for OMIG's size, thinking the simplicity of it would be appealing and easier to move forward with. However, in further conversation with Ohio Mutual, they agreed that they should both have skin in the game around the success of their efforts and worked to structure a deal that ensured neither party lost when the other one won. It had to be mutually risky and mutually attractive at the same time.

OMIG worked with their analytics team and proposed a model to cover basic costs of the project, while creating upside for Pinpoint based on actual results. While they needed to negotiate the specifics to the satisfaction of both sides, the concept was appealing to Pinpoint, too, and the companies arrived at a mutually agreeable pricing model and signed an agreement in March.

They couldn't simply go live then, though, as OMIG had decided that they would use summer interns to work with the survey vendor on the results, so they would have to wait for those resources to be in place. That also meant Pinpoint would need to run their model later to be sure it had the most up-to-date view of insureds and was being applied to the most relevant view of OMIG's in-force homeowners' book. OMIG pulled their data in April, and Pinpoint gave them the results in May (today, this is fully automated, with turnaround time of just a few short hours). By that point, Pinpoint's refinements to the model had increased the spread from top to bottom decile to 44x, making it even more accurate and powerful.

OMIG decided to focus on the top decile for this first effort because of how strongly positive the indication of owning a wood-burning stove was. The model flagged roughly 2,000 homes in the riskiest decile as likely having unreported stoves, which OMIG sent to their survey vendor to mail to. This represented 28% of the top decile as likely owning a wood-burning stove.

> "The interesting thing is what you're not usually expecting."
>
> – Avi Tuschman
> Founder & CIO,
> Pinpoint Predictive

Through the double mailing and phone-call follow-up, the vendor achieved a 76% response rate (1,521), of which roughly 20% (314 homes) reported having a wood-burning stove that Ohio Mutual was not aware of. They then dug in deeper to understand more about the stoves; offer guidance and action to the insured to make the risk acceptable; rate the risk for the stove at renewal; or, when it could not be made acceptable (for example, a homemade stove OMIG found to be located in a garage where gasoline was also being stored), the risk was non-renewed.

Agents were aware at every step of the process, and Roderick and Combs confirmed that things were relatively quiet with agents. Three agents said they did not want to have their insureds participate at this time, and OMIG decided to honor that request.

Ohio Mutual said they learned several things about their insureds and wood-burning stove usage by doing this project beyond just the surprise of 300+ stoves they were not aware of. These learnings specifically came because of their decision to do this for renewals and not new business.

If they had done this on new business, they would have found one or two wood-burning stoves at a time, given the way new business comes in. It can be hard to see patterns in data that drips in like this, coming to different underwriters each time. But because they did this in bulk, as their renewal focus afforded, they immediately saw patterns in the types of stoves people had, the reactions to their suggestions, and how that varied by geography.

With a book focused on the Midwest and New England, OMIG saw clear differences in the regions. Their discovering the need to change the language around calling them wood-burning versus solid fuel stoves was directly from seeing how New Englanders interpreted "wood-burning" literally, while Midwesterners seemed to understand the more liberal meaning OMIG intended. They also saw differences in likelihood to have built the stove yourself rather than buying a commercial solution, and whether you self-installed and maintain or had a professional install and clean it. They found differences in how agents engaged in the program, as well. All of this led to unanticipated additional value to OMIG and adjustments in how they approach these markets.

The teams at both companies took away several learnings and insights from the experience more specific to working together and innovating.

> "I think you're going to have to find something a little bit different to win, and if you don't, someone else will."
>
> – Chad Combs
> VP, Personal Lines,
> Ohio Mutual

One of the things that stood out to me most was how seemingly obscure the use case was, and how you would ever stumble across something like this. In fact, it was not obscure for Pinpoint. Their solution looks for drivers of greatest impact from the sea of possibilities in an insurer's data. It can be easy for people living in the business every day to overlook opportunities like this that exist within our own data but are hard to see without the right tools or perspective. Given the potential value here, it seems like finding a way to shine a light on applications people wouldn't normally consider is critical. Tuschman said of this wood-burning stove application, "The interesting thing is what you're not usually expecting. We're investors in a sense. It's a scientific process where you're trying to understand cause and effect, and we need to think about where we should invest to find that."

He also noted the need to work with partners who care deeply about solving these issues, and how important it is to work with those who are responsible for the actual function or business you're hoping to impact. He said of the team at Ohio Mutual, "There's an intrinsic enthusiasm, and they truly care not only about the business, but also the individuals being insured. Ohio Mutual understands the potential of using technology like AI to serve their clients better, and they're acutely aware that there's unpriceable risk, and a need to solve for that."

Shannon Shallcross, Head of Customer Success at Pinpoint, added that you must be willing to "think outside of the constraints of how we've always done it," and that the team at OMIG had this willingness.

Combs reflected from OMIG's side, starting with the initial way the solution struggled to find an application and make progress. "You can get into letting things linger as you get in the habit of the day to day, but there is value to recognizing that and taking definitive action on things so you can move on to what's next rather than being stuck with a number of things in process but not happening."

He sees a general lack of proactivity in things like this, and said:

> "It's kind of like a disease. There's something here, so how do we make it work? We have to do it the right way and look to our guiding principles, of course. Lack of action is a strategy – but a losing strategy. Don't just do things to do things, but don't be so scared to do anything that you get beat. There are so many cool things happening right now that we didn't have before. That takes building a different muscle from the 'don't rock the boat' way we did things to be successful before. I think you're going to have to find something a little bit different to win, and if you don't, someone else will."

Foundations for The Future

- A lack of clarity on use case or applicability can be ok, but you need to have a path to finding it quickly to keep projects from languishing.

- Build agility into your approach to contracting as much as development and project management. Size your contracts and their complexity for the scale of what's in front of you and avoid the urge to over-contract for a given stage of the journey.

- Include your legal resources in your business case so they can be more effective on contract negotiations given their better understanding of the context, details, and intentions all around.

- Finding ways to limit disruption can allow shorter time-to-market and reduce potential change management risk. After something is proven, you can look to making further improvements or change because people will be bought into what you're doing while trusting you to do it reasonably and without disrupting their lives as much as they may otherwise have feared.

- Being concerned about new approaches or solutions, like AI, can be understandable. Rather than sitting on the sidelines, look for ways to learn more about them through smart application of the technology so you have a potential competitive advantage once they take hold rather than having to play catch up to competitors who are far ahead of you.

7. American European Insurance Group & Protosure

For many carriers who still rely on mainframe systems, they find themselves between a rock and a hard place.

Starting with the hard place, market pressures demand being able to transact electronically, quickly and without asking people to break the way they work to accommodate how you work. Your products and rates need to keep pace with the industry, even if your systems make updating existing or introducing new products a complex and lengthy process that always leaves you behind competitive offerings.

These legacy systems make accommodating market demands difficult and expensive at best, or impossible at worst. Either the systems do not seem capable of enabling any of the needed modern ways of working, or the perceived cost of doing so becomes a non-starter.

For carriers who have committed to modernizing their systems, that too creates a complication as they freeze development on legacy systems or shun potential throw-away investment in interim solutions while they wait for their new systems to be ready. That can result in multiple years of exacerbation of the problem they find themselves in.

This is the rock – a large, seemingly immovable barrier carriers can feel crushed against when facing the hard place of market demands.

There is hope, though. A new generation of technologies like cloud-based solutions, the explosion of API-driven tools and more flexible, nimble coding approaches have breathed new life into mainframe systems and can do so at much lower cost and shorter timeframes than was ever possible.

Ironically, that last characteristic – being cheaper and faster – has led some carriers to shun such solutions out of fear that they aren't robust enough to deliver on their promises or are simply too good to be true. After decades of being trained to see IT projects as expensive and slow, something that is neither of those things seems like it cannot be trusted (problematically, we also have trouble trusting the big, expensive, slow solutions because we have been burned by them in the past). Adding to this, many of these newer solutions come from very young companies, setting off our risk averse radars as to the viability of such offerings and the chance the company behind them will be in business long enough to deliver (or support what they deliver if they do survive long enough).

This is the context in which two companies ended up coming together: American European Insurance Group (AEIG) and Protosure.

AEIG is a New York-based writer of personal property lines (Homeowners, Renters, Condo) and small commercial lines (BOP, Package, Umbrella, Contractors, Commercial Auto and Habitational). A small, privately-owned carrier with a defined geographic footprint, the cost of moving on from the AS/400 mainframe system they ran on always seemed hard to justify, and yet market pressures continued to increase the need to do so.

In updating one of their existing products in the mid-2010s, the time and cost involved in creating the new screens on their legacy agent portal became the final straw for the company, and they decided they needed to figure out a solution.

Schlomo Neumann, an accountant by training with responsibilities in Finance at AEIG, became VP of Operations and took responsibility for IT, which was largely focused on the maintenance of the AS/400 infrastructure. He saw a need to bring in additional perspective and talent that was versed in more modern engineering approaches and recruited a new team member right out of undergrad, Raphael Breuer. Breuer was tasked with looking at ways to help AEIG's agents do business more easily with the carrier, while helping to identify ways to navigate the tricky path ahead around their core system situation.

By this time, agents were used to interacting with carriers through portals for real-time quoting, binding and payment and connecting to insurer systems from within their agency management systems. When carriers could not support such approaches, agents started to view these carriers almost as markets of last resort because of the time and effort needed to do business with them. Agents would go to carriers that could quickly and effortlessly offer quotes and would only turn to those who took manual effort and days to quote rather than minutes if they absolutely had to. AEIG did not want this to be their reality yet were unsure how to stop that from happening while they found a path forward for their core system and brought a new one online. That process of solving things at the root level would surely take longer than AEIG had before this fate befell them.

It was still early days of InsurTech, and much of the talk was around things like disruptive new insurers, drones, IoT and other things that Neumann didn't see as applying to what AEIG needed to solve for. Despite that, he and Breuer attended an early insurtech event put on by Insurance Insider in NYC in the summer of 2018 where Protosure founder and CEO, Urijah Kaplan, happened to be attending, having just completed a prototype of their solution.

For Kaplan and the team at Protosure, while they were a new company with no customers, this was actually nothing new to them. He and others on the team had started an MGA in 2008 with a supplemental unemployment insurance offering and had to build a system to run the MGA that could work with the legacy systems of their fronting carrier, Great American. After Great American bought the MGA, Kaplan and the team became a software firm supporting the system for their former fronting carrier, who became their sole client.

From that first contract, they expanded their offering in 2013, and became the system one of the top five P&C carriers used for their exclusive agents to place Homeowners risks with other markets when that carrier couldn't take them – a solution that is still in place today.

Through this experience, Kaplan and the team started to see the same dilemma AEIG, and others faced. They thought about building a policy administration system to solve it but realized it would be very hard to convince insurers to buy such a critical system from a brand new, small company, and the development costs and sales cycles for core systems are generally too high and too long for startups to survive. Instead, they thought about how new technology and approaches could enable a lightweight solution that could be dropped on top of or alongside a legacy system to breathe new life into it rather than trying to replace it. The term "no-code" had not emerged yet, but that is what they envisioned – a no-code, drag and drop solution for building and deploying products and interfaces to the market quickly and effectively at zero marginal cost.

They named their new company Protosure on the idea of allowing insurers to almost create prototype insurance products they could essentially "try before they buy", meaning they can easily get it into the market before having to really spend any money to do so.

Having lived with the problem themselves, the team saw how it could take a year or more to be able to launch a new product, with changes taking months to implement as they queue up behind other priorities. Product innovation can end up taking years to reach the market even though the new idea had long since been developed.

Kaplan was talking to someone at the event about what they were building, and Breuer overheard the conversation, and joined in. He was intrigued and started to ask Kaplan more questions about what they were doing and how it might apply to what AEIG was thinking about. Breuer shared what he heard with Neumann, and they invited Kaplan to the offices the next week to hear more about their needs, share a demo of Protosure, and see if there might be a possibility to work together.

Neumann, Breuer and others at AEIG quickly saw how Protosure would have saved them two to three weeks for each iterative change of the product they had just updated, adding up to a significant increase in release speed across the project. They also saw that Protosure would not solve their ultimate need to modernize their core system, but what it would do is buy them the time and space to figure that out while protecting the business from being marginalized by their agents. With Protosure, they could enable online quote, bind and payment via an agent portal, update existing products and launch new ones while still feeding their AS/400 system everything it needed for them to operate the company.

This all sounded good; however, they faced a few complications in the decision-making process.

Since it was clear that Protosure was not going to be their new policy administration system, and they would still need to buy and implement something new, any investment in Protosure's solution would be thrown away eventually. It was, in essence, a Band-Aid or workaround rather than the real solution. Neumann said they dealt with this issue by looking at the economics of it rather than trying to get too philosophical about spending on something they ultimately would likely stop using. The cost of working with Protosure was low, the benefits were clear and high, so even if they stopped using it after a couple of years, it would still make good financial sense to move forward.

Another complication came from one of the things that made the economics so attractive. Protosure was inexpensive relative to what AEIG was used to seeing, and they were a brand new, small company with no customers in production. What if they failed or ran out of runway before delivering on what AEIG needed? Or what if they survived, but their size and newness meant they were not really up to the task they were promising to complete or were too naïve to understand the complexities they faced? Protosure did not have years of successful deployments with multiple insurers to prove their idea out or give confidence of their delivery capabilities, and with no existing live customers, there were no references to check.

Neumann again turned to the economics. The risk, which was a mix of the cost of the contract and the fact that none of their core systems or processes would be impacted or changed, was low. Even if they got nothing in the end, the real impact on their business was small enough that they felt it warranted trying. And in that attempt, their people may grow and develop in a way they would not have gotten a chance to otherwise, bringing more value to the company, which alone may make the financial risk worth it.

Neumann does credit AEIG's size, private ownership and structure with their ability to make decisions this way. He said, "Not every carrier could do what we did because of the structure and decision matrix they have to go through. We just look at whether the cost and benefit are right. We don't need to evaluate for years."

While he's right that they have an inherent advantage in this regard, there is also nothing standing in the way of any insurer, big or small, making decisions this way. AEIG may be set up to do so more easily, but this ability is not unique to AEIG, and insurers like them.

Neumann added another potential factor for him specifically, given that he was relatively new to insurance and didn't have years of Insurance-specific IT project difficulties behind him. "I was very new to projects like this, which was probably to my benefit, because I wasn't jaded or framed with other concerns."

For the startup survival risk specifically, AEIG leaned on the impression Kaplan made, his prior track record and that of the team, and the clear understanding Protosure had, not just of their technology but the context into which it was being deployed because they had lived it themselves.[4] This didn't change the risks of the realities of startup survivability but gave AEIG some mitigating comfort. They also realized that companies could fail completely or fail to deliver what they promised at any age.

> "We don't have to do something the way the industry does it. Things don't have to cost so much or be as complicated as we can make them."
>
> – Schlomo Neumann
> VP, Operations,
> American European
> Insurance Group

From my experience at a startup, I recall some sales conversations where carriers had specific rules as to how old a vendor must be before they could sign a contract with them. One C-suite executive I was presenting to asked me how long we had been in business, and I told him this was our second-year operating. He said, unfortunately, their CEO had a rule that no vendor that is less than 12 years old could be used, so we should stop the meeting there despite the solution looking like it would meet their needs and work well. I remember wondering how many companies failed in year 11 versus year 13, or whether there was any rationale to the CEO's decision on needing a dozen years. I also wondered whether company age could ever be a liability, but also that none of this would change their minds. Our main competitor at the time had several years on us (eight versus our two), and now, four years later, has exited the insurance market and was shut down after being acquired while the company I worked for is going strong. This would have been that competitor's twelfth year in business. Had that CEO's rule forced that carrier to go into business with that competitor, they

---

[4] As the timing of this story was pre-COVID, Neumann said that would have created some additional concern as to whether Protosure would survive, but, again, the economics and scale of risk were not such that their decision needed to change.

would have quickly found themselves in trouble by picking the vendor that met the rule instead of the one who was only halfway there.[5]

This is another example of the kind of thing Neumann was speaking to when recognizing how AEIG can make decisions differently because of their situation. And, again, making ROI and relative-risk-based decisions need not be unique to AEIG, nor does it necessarily protect you from risk, as my personal example shows.

All of this said, AEIG did not go forward blindly with Protosure. They had also looked at other options from more established companies. What they found was more heft in those options, but not necessarily more benefit. Those solutions required multiple year SaaS license commitments, subscriptions to data services, etc. All of that made the cost side of the decision matrix heavier without commensurately improving the benefit side (or decreasing it due to the slower deployment and change speed), giving Protosure an edge despite the risks of being a newer company.

The simplicity of the proposed solution and low relative cost also meant negotiations and contracting were uneventful. Again, this is something industry players sometimes over-engineer even in simple situations. Neumann said of his approach, "We don't have to do something the way the industry does it. Things don't have to cost so much or be as complicated as we can make them."

The only real back and forth on the agreement was to make sure everyone understood things clearly on both sides so there would be no surprises, scope issues, or other avoidable complications. As we see in other stories here, contracting can be a time to ensure shared understanding rather than winning points.

> "The thought is, if you have a legacy system, you're stuck. No."
>
> – Schlomo Neumann
> VP, Operations,
> American European
> Insurance Group

From that first meeting at the conference in July 2018, the two companies were ready to move forward by the end of the summer. Work started somewhat slowly as AEIG did not have any IT resource exclusively dedicated to the Protosure work and had to get some other

---

[5] Incidentally, that carrier still has not deployed any bi-directional texting solution, possibly because there are no 12-year-old options to choose from.

things in place first, including building the agent portal Protosure would operate within.

Once the portal was developed, things started to move faster, and the two companies saw a need to be able to communicate more directly. They setup a Slack workspace in May 2019, which really helped by cutting out any delays in communication that can be so typical in a dynamic engineering situation involving separate companies.

By July, the solution was live with AEIG's Habitational coverage, and without any crises or setbacks during development and deployment. Since it was agent facing, AEIG wanted to ensure everything was ready and thoroughly tested. They always wanted sufficient time to train agents, which is part of why the project took the time it did. Otherwise, there were no major issues contributing to the time involved. Still, going from that first overheard conversation at a conference to being in production in one year is quite fast – especially when you consider the context of a presumed inability to do anything because of the constraints of mainframe systems.

After deploying the Habitational product, AEIG had two more products they wanted to release on Protosure. For one, a Mercantile coverage, they decided not to move forward due to their focus on a general system upgrade and hardening in the market making the immediate need for something like what they did in Habitational irrelevant. Agent demand for fast, easy quotes was no longer there, meaning it wasn't worth the effort to move that product to Protosure, no matter how easy it would be.

The other product, Homeowners, was able to be released with no assistance from Protosure staff, really proving out the vision Kaplan and the team had for the simplicity and self-deployment they wanted to create in their solution.

While it solved an immediate need, more strategically, this allowed AEIG to look for a long-term solution for their core systems without undue pressure from the market that might otherwise lead them to make a rushed, sub-optimal or compromised decision. As Neumann sees it, Protosure bought AEIG several years they didn't otherwise have to be in market with a new core system. They've recently announced that plan with their selected core system provider and expect to move on from their Protosure solution when that is ready.

Ironically, knowing the investment will stop paying dividends in the near future, Neumann is perhaps even *more* positive on it today because of how much more their Protosure project did for them than they expected. Not only did it give them the time they needed, protect them from being marginalized in the agent channel, and let them update products or launch new ones, he sees how it has helped AEIG to change as a company. He said, "We have evolved since we went live and are more software-focused than we used to be." No doubt, this has prepared better them for their new core system journey.

He said that their underwriters now know that, if they need a change, IT can say yes to it, and get it done quickly. That flexibility gave AEIG the ability to better understand what's important and what they need from a system, which helped inform their selection of a new core system.

It also helped reinforce the importance of not just being great underwriters working offline or with outdated systems that create friction for the market or being a tech-forward company with limited underwriting expertise. You cannot be at either extreme and win, in Neumann's eyes. This project helped them to better understand how to balance the two to create a successful underwriting company that is enabled by their technology to be flexible and responsive.

For the industry, Neumann shares some parting wisdom in the realization AEIG had that many can benefit from. He said:

> "The thought is, if you have a legacy system, you're stuck. No. Protosure gave us the ability to meet the market. Even if it wasn't the flashiest thing at the time, it was the right tool because it gave us the capabilities we needed in a straight forward way that let us do what we needed to do efficiently and confidently."

Foundations for The Future

- If the ROI makes sense, that can drive decision making even when philosophical barriers may exist, like a solution being throw-away or a stop-gap measure.

- Risk is relative rather than absolute. Even if an effort fails, the impact of the failure may be relatively small, and there may be other benefits to trying, such as staff learning and developing, that more than make up for it.

- Take a right-sized, risk-based approach as you evaluate options and move ahead through contracting, development, implementation, etc. If the scale of the risk is not material, recognize that in how you negotiate contract wording, the depth of due diligence you do, and other ways you increase cost and complexity that may not align with the situation. Just because you do it elsewhere, doesn't mean you have to do it everywhere (or that what you're doing elsewhere should even be done there!).

- Legacy systems can complicate innovation and progress but need not be seen as immovable rocks that limit any and all progress. New tools and approaches exist today that can unlock possibility in areas that would have been unimaginable just a few years ago.

8. Homesteaders Life & Benekiva

For any company, it can be hard to balance having a collaborative, non-hierarchical and transparent culture across people and functions while also maintaining clear ownership and responsibility. I've worked at hierarchy-free organizations where everyone had a voice, making it hard to get things done since we always needed to pull together huge groups of people to agree to anything. And I've seen command-and-control styles where people were told what to think and admonished if they had the audacity to veer outside their area of direct responsibility.

In a startup, striking this balance is even more critical as you have to ensure everyone is pulling in the same direction and contributing everything they possibly can. Most startups really stress their culture and collaborative, open spirit where every voice matters. Yet, they also need to ensure they get things done and deliver effectively. When the poison of mistrust or the suppression of good ideas sets in, it can be hard for everyone to contribute in the way startups need them to. And when no clear decision owner exists for each of the many critical moments a startup faces, timelines extend, missteps get made, and runway runs out.

The need to create this balance can be heightened as soon as customers are brought into the mix. Startups will face new pressures as their often-rare sources of revenue and product feedback will sometimes create influence to veer off the right path for the startup.

If you are trying to build something transformational for an industry, a specific customer with specific needs may try to push you away from your bigger goal to meet what they believe is more important or is at least more important to them in that moment. Often, that thing may be a quirk of their business, a vestige of how they have worked historically, or the whim of someone with political clout at that customer. While their idea may be right, it isn't right simply by virtue of it coming from them. And customers, especially large or early ones, may try to use their leverage to get the startup to do what they want.

This dynamic can repeat itself with investors since, after all, they are paying for what the startup is doing. If they believe something should be done a certain way, they could exert leverage or influence to ensure it is. This can happen subconsciously or inadvertently, with investors sharing ideas with founders who then feel like they have to do what their investor suggested since there's a sense of indebtedness to those who funded the company. That new idea may be the right answer, but it needs to be done *because* it's right and not merely because the people with the purse strings were its source.

In that way, extending the lines of clear responsibility to customer and investor relationships is perhaps even more critical for a startup than defining responsibilities internally. And in today's world where more and more insurers are becoming investors in addition to customers, the impact of ill-defined lines of responsibility runs the risk of having dramatic negative consequences for startups.

That is the underlying story behind the building of Benekiva, and their relationship with their first customer who also became their first investor, Homesteaders Life Company (HLC).

For Benekiva, defining what they called 'lanes' for each of the three founders has been critical to allowing them to execute effectively while also pushing for transparency and inclusion on a daily basis. It also ensured they could engage with their first customer and investor in a way that supported their goal of changing how claims are handled in the Life insurance market and beyond.

In P&C insurance, many people go their entire life never having a claim. They (luckily) never end up in a situation where they need to call upon the coverage they paid for and are left having paid for peace of mind rather than needing help putting their life back together after a loss.

With Life insurance, things are a bit different in that everyone ends up in the exact situation they bought coverage for. Of course, there are term policies that people outlive, and therefore never have to make a claim on, but every life ends, so ultimately you would expect a near-100% claim rate for whole and other types of Life policies.

Yet, in 2010, Brent Williams, Founder and CEO of Benekiva, heard a statistic while at a conference that roughly two-thirds of all Life insurance policies go unclaimed. He remembers thinking it was so high that it must be wrong.

But it wasn't.

Having been a veteran of the space, Williams knew that insurers do not try to get out of paying valid claims, so this low claim rate isn't because carriers are trying to skirt their responsibility (contrary to popular opinion). Instead, he wondered what was getting in the way of people's survivors getting the benefits that were envisioned for them when a policy was taken out.

As he kept exploring the issue, he realized there were several factors, one of which seemed like it could be solved through new ways of thinking of claim systems and processes, giving birth to the idea for Benekiva.

For years, Life insurance claim systems had been overlooked as investment went to underwriting and sales system to drive policy acquisition and retention. The result was that the industry had claims tools that were woefully behind the times and the need, yielding cumbersome, archaic beneficiary and employee experiences, which contributed to slower claim payment at best, or abandoned or unfiled claims at worst.

While still in their day jobs, Williams joined forces with fellow co-founders, Bobbie and Soven Shrivastav, to work through the idea for how a better claim system could enable insurers to more easily provide the protection they intended for the beneficiaries of their insureds.

The trio refined the idea and began work on a prototype system, still keeping their day jobs while they worked to deliver something they thought an insurer would be able to use. The plan was to have a fully functioning solution they could put into production with a carrier, learn more, refine their offering, and grow from there.

The problem they faced was a chicken and egg situation, or perhaps even a catch 22. For an insurer to work with them, the three needed to be able to point to successful deployments and tangible ROIs, but they couldn't do either of those things without a carrier being willing to be the first to sign on. And, because of that conundrum, the team continued to work on Benekiva as a side hustle.

In early 2017, through his connections from being in the Life insurer space in Des Moines, Iowa, Williams secured a meeting with

Steve Lang, then-CEO of Homesteaders Life. Williams shared what he believed to be the problem in the industry, and how he and the Shrivastavs were trying to solve it.

After a couple of meetings, Lang was intrigued, but had a blocker to his ability to be more interested in doing something – his impending retirement. Lang introduced Williams to his successor, HLC's COO, Steve Shaffer, who had come from outside the industry having held various leadership roles in private equity-backed enterprises. Shaffer would soon be taking the helm at HLC and had a strong desire to move the organization's culture to be more innovative and agile. He was intrigued by what working with a startup could do to help in that endeavor, and also saw how the issue Benekiva was trying to solve was one HLC faced, making this a good potential opportunity to move the 115-plus-year-old insurer forward.

Unlike other Life insurers that drove the unbelievable stat that sparked William's initial idea, HLC, who sells pre-need funeral expense coverage, sees roughly 100% of claims paid. So, while they did not struggle with valid claims going unclaimed or unpaid, they certainly faced the same issue others in the industry did around the pain of handling those claims and processing payments. That meant Shaffer saw a direct need at HLC for the kind of solution Williams was proposing, but he also saw the benefit as greater for other kinds of insurers than for HLC.

This could have been a reason to pass on having further conversations with Benekiva, but it meant something else to Shaffer. Rather than confining the benefits case for HLC to what they would directly gain with a better claim system, he realized there would be great upside if HLC could benefit from the industry-level potential Benekiva represented, and he was interested in being both a customer *and* investor.

On the customer side, HLC had a system that did what they needed, but was hard to change and would often break when they tried to change it, resulting in longer project times, higher cost, and less flexibility than they wished they had. While it didn't stop their business, it was a constraining force and source of pain that would be better to operate without. As Shaffer and his team looked at what Benekiva had built so far, and where they planned to take it, they realized it would solve the things HLC was hoping to address.

On the investment side, HLC had recently brought in a new Head of Claims from another insurer and heard from her and others on her team that had come from outside that the issues HLC faced were not unique to them. Employee after employee recounted facing the same struggles at carriers they had worked at before, confirming to Shaffer that the market potential Benekiva talked about was real.

However, that confirmation alone doesn't mean Benekiva was positioned to seize on that opportunity. Evaluating that likelihood meant scanning the market to understand if others were addressing it, and what kind of competitive threat they posed to Benekiva. Luckily, HLC would need to scan the market whether they were considering investing or not for their decision to be a customer of Benekiva since they wanted to see if there were viable alternatives available – especially ones that were actually in business with proven track records rather than being a group of three part-time founders with other jobs.

From the initial conversation Williams had with Lang at the start of the year, HLC had come to some conclusions about six months later. What they found is that Benekiva could meet their needs, other carriers faced the same problems, and no one else was addressing these issues sufficiently, if at all.

The one area they saw competition for Benekiva was internally, with their technology team believing they could build something that would do what Benekiva proposed. While Shaffer had faith his people could do this, he also realized there would be barriers to timely success if they took a 'build' path. First, the other priorities the IT department faced meant it would likely be several years before they could produce something similar to what Benekiva had already built. Second, on his desire to move the culture of the organization, Shaffer realized working with a startup could help his team move their mindset and approach to change in a way that doing the project internally likely wouldn't. And in these realizations, he saw how home built competition to Benekiva also did not pose a credible enough threat to the market opportunity to suggest it being a material risk to Benekiva's overall potential and attractiveness as an investment.

Everything seemed to point clearly to moving forward with Benekiva as a system provider to HLC and to considering investing, except one lingering concern – startup risk. How would HLC be impacted if Benekiva failed as a company? And to be fair, Benekiva almost wasn't a company in the first place since the founders still had day jobs, amplifying the sense of riskiness.

To work through this, Shaffer broke the problem into two pieces. First, if Benekiva did not survive, HLC would be left with a claim system they owned, as they would have if they had built it in-house. In this sense, they would be no worse off than the only reasonable alternative to going with Benekiva, which was building it themselves. And they would likely end up with this system from a defunct startup faster than if they built it themselves, so this 'failure' scenario would actually still be a win for HLC.

On the risk around the founders not being all-in, Shaffer was clear with Williams and Bobbie Shrivastav that they had to quit their jobs and do this full time if they wanted HLC as a customer, investor or both. He didn't need to ask this of Soven, who had already quit his job to work as Benekiva's CTO full-time. That is, if HLC was taking a chance on Benekiva, the founders had to take the chance on *themselves* and demonstrate their commitment to HLC's success as much as Benekiva's.

Of course, Bobbie and Brent wanted to do this, and were excited to have the clarity that they could now take the leap they had been waiting to take. Shaffer added, jokingly, that he also thought they were crazy for leaving their jobs, as a bit of a nod to the risk averse nature of insurance mindsets.

Both sides were on board on the idea of moving ahead with the two aspects of the partnership, but still had a lot of details to work out before they could. Now came the time to negotiate the commercial terms for HLC becoming a customer of Benekiva's SaaS system and those for it becoming an investor in the startup.

The commercial negotiation was relatively straight forward, with the focus really being on everyone truly understanding what was to be built, how it would be delivered, and everyone's responsibilities and expectations. This was, in effect, putting on paper the kind of lanes of responsibility that the two companies would come to rely on to ensure a successful delivery of Benekiva's system.

The investment specifics took greater nuance and consideration, though. With his PE experience, Shaffer knew that the way the investment was structured could enable great things for Benekiva (and HLC as its sole investor at the time) or be a deadweight dragging Benekiva down, potentially to its doom.

Shaffer realized that it was important for the founders to maintain control of the company to ensure it can focus on its ultimate opportunity (beyond just HLC's needs), yet Benekiva would need a sizeable investment to deliver on its potential, which would require giving up a lot of equity for this pre-revenue startup. The solution was for HLC to make a big enough investment for the founders to commit full-time and hire the team they needed to start to deliver for HLC as a customer, but not more than that. This meant Benekiva did not have to give up too much equity while their valuation was still low.

While that would address the equity and control concerns, it created a new issue by raising runway risk for Benekiva since it gave them little breathing room and meant the founders would need to raise funds again soon. For anyone who has been in an early-stage startup, you know how time-consuming fundraising can be, and how it can take so much of the founders' time that everything else grinds to a halt. This obviously wouldn't be good for Benekiva, but also would be a threat to HLC's initial investment, so Shaffer knew more work was needed on the right overall approach.

The answer was for the investment to come in a staged structure that would trigger additional investments as key strategic milestones that would increase Benekiva's valuation had been reached. This was a major unlock for both sides.

For Benekiva, they would still get the overall funding they believed they needed, but it would come through multiple, subsequent investments that would be cheaper from an equity standpoint than if they had been made up front at a lower valuation. This protected the founders' control while also ensuring funds would be there as they needed them. And it meant the founders didn't need to pause running the business to go fund raise when runway was running out. The investment structure also specifically allowed the founders the time to do sales rather than fundraising, saving the company from having to recruit and build a sales team for the first several years.

This approach allowed Benekiva some of the valuation and equity benefits of bootstrapping while also enabling similar levels of growth as would be possible with venture funding while saving them the overhead of having to do that fundraising.

For HLC, the staged approach provided some financial protection, which was helpful for Shaffer in getting board support for making an investment like this, which was a first for HLC. Had they poured the full investment into Benekiva up front, then the entire amount would be at risk, making the investment decision much trickier for the board to support and getting approval a much more involved process for Shaffer.

Shaffer said of the approach, "We structured the deal to be firing bullets instead of shooting cannons. That gave Benekiva what they needed, but also limited the risk to HLC at every stage."

> "We structured the deal to be firing bullets instead of shooting cannons."
>
> – Steve Shaffer
> CEO, Homesteaders Life Company

An alternate approach of being a limited partner in a bigger fund could have also provided HLC protection through diversification but would rob them of the direct experience and exposure they would get by working with the company they invested in as closely as they would with Benekiva.

Many investors might have simply wanted to maximize their equity position, making this approach seem contrary to HLC's best interest. However, Shaffer realized that there was a risk that HLC effectively owning Benekiva would smother the company, keeping it from reaching the true market potential it could otherwise realize. As its owner, HLC could push Benekiva to build what HLC needed rather than what the market needed. That would seemingly make Benekiva a better fit for HLC's immediate need, and a worse fit for future customers, weakening their chance of success.

And, if HLC owned Benekiva effectively or in actuality, Benekiva would inherently have to slow down to HLC's corporate pace, even if only slightly. Startups can fail in the time they have to wait for monthly decision-making meetings, quarterly board decisions, etc., so Shaffer knew Benekiva needed to remain independent of that to succeed.

But it went further than this. Shaffer and the Benekiva team also realized that this would help protect them against a common mistake carriers make when putting in new systems. As discussed elsewhere in this book, we often end up rebuilding the old ways of working when putting in new tools rather than allowing these new systems to move us forward operationally and experientially. If Benekiva was too closed off to other input and ideas or could not provide push back or challenge to HLC because they were being managed as subservient to their owners, both companies would suffer.

In fact, this mentality extended from the investment decision to the customer decision and structure. The leaders at both companies realized they had to separate oversight of the two relationships to ensure there never came moments where one was used to pressure the other. You can easily imagine a case where any questions or problems on the delivery side could be used as leverage on the investment side, or *vice versa* where your main investor could push you to do something for them as your customer because they were funding you.

To that end, the project steering committee was comprised of key leaders from across HLC, including Claims and IT, but not Shaffer. Instead, Shaffer met monthly with Benekiva's founders to discuss the strategy and trajectory of the business, while drawing a clear line they would not cross over by discussing minutiae or problems in the work for HLC.

Had HLC only been a customer, it would have been wise and appropriate for Shaffer to be on the steering committee, but because of the dual relationship and Shaffer's criticality on the investment side of it, he made a conscious decision to delineate and separate his responsibilities to protect both companies.

This mirrored how Williams and the Shrivastavs ran Benekiva from the start, with clear lanes and responsibilities. They wanted to be collaborative and inclusive, but also knew that, despite each of them having views on the areas the other two ran, there would always be a clear decision maker for each aspect of the business. Bobbie Shrivastav, who is COO, owned the operational, product, project management and customer aspects of the business. Soven Shrivastav, CTO, owned engineering and technical delivery. Brent Williams, as CEO, had overall strategic and management responsibility, as well as leading Sales. For example, if there was a technical decision to be made, while Bobbie and Brent would have input into the matter, Soven would make the ultimate decision and Bobbie and Brent would support it, knowing they had input into that decision, and it was considered seriously and meaningfully along the way.

They knew that they had to start the company in such a collaborative style paired with clear ownership, and then defend this key cultural and structural approach as they grew to roughly 100 people over the course of this story. And the same was true for their relationship with HLC to ensure success on both sides.

These clear lanes were tested early on as delivery work began. HLC staff had a lot of functionality they felt was required because it was part of how the company had worked before. When Benekiva did not immediately embrace these requests because they believed they would hold HLC and the solution back from more efficient processes and better customer and employee experiences, some at HLC became uncomfortable. Shaffer recalls early on that he would hear from people who wondered why they couldn't just make Benekiva do what they wanted since they 'owned them'. He reminded them that wasn't the structure, and that he wasn't going to use their investment as leverage in working through those matters.

Instead, the responsibility sat with that team and Benekiva through their project governance structure. Bobbie Shrivastav recalls the early flood of requests like these, and HLC's staff's initial expectations that they would all just be taken in and delivered. Through their regular communication and meeting cadence, they could review the requests together, and step back from solutionizing and instead think about business outcomes.

Shrivastav recalls, "Initially, they would come to us with a request, what outcome they needed, and would even provide wireframes of how it should work." They worked together to change the interaction and refocus the HLC team solely on the outcome rather than the "how" behind it. This is part of the kind of cultural change Shaffer was hoping to see come from the work together.

Part of that shift came from the way Benekiva instituted regular retrospectives on each sprint in the project. They came together with the team from HLC to share what went well, what needed improvement and what should be stopped all together. This is a normal part of Agile development, but also something that's foreign to many organizations. Or they do it, but it's more one sided or is met with resistance from whichever side is getting the feedback.

Benekiva made a point to share feedback with HLC and push to get it back so that it was a two-way street. They established rules of engagement in a sense by role modeling how they received HLC's feedback to set the tone for the sessions. Bobbie Shrivastav led the sessions, and spoke about the humility, trust and comfort everyone had as it became clear through regular, repeated retrospectives that people were being honest and reasonable in what they shared and were open to what they were hearing.

This paid dividends in the day to day working of the teams by shifting the cultural norms around feedback being safe and necessary rather than a euphemism for criticism or a function of the performance management process.

Benekiva actually expanded this approach by making it part of their annual customer conference. They hold open retrospective sessions with customers in attendance and invite prospects to the event to listen. For the uninitiated, it can be almost shocking to watch customers share what they wish was different or better in front of prospects you might think Benekiva would only want to show purely positive or sanitized things to. But for the founders, they believe showing this honest view and how they receive it *is* a positive thing about Benekiva and has been a critical part of how they've been successful with the customers they work with.

One specific issue they faced with HLC came as the project started to hit snags and slow down. HLC had a third-party consultant engaged as the main conduit between the business and Benekiva on requirements. Benekiva noticed some requirements and push back from HLC on things that seemed unusual or extremely rare that were being framed as critical or must-have functionality for the initial go-live.

They worked to better understand the issues and see if they truly were must-haves. As they did, they found that these were extremely rare, edge cases that could be solved for other ways or in future releases and did not appear to be showstoppers for an initial go-live. For example, one such issue occurred 28 times out of over 65,000 claims paid a year at HLC at the time (or less than 0.004% of the time). Yet the consultant kept insisting that they were showstoppers and pushed for the project to be delayed to get them delivered before launch.

The HLC project team was frustrated not to have the functionality they were being told they must have by their consultant, and also that the project was slowing down due to this.

Benekiva was frustrated as they wanted to see the project move forward and were having trouble understanding why these particular issues were holding that up when they couldn't see the criticality for HLC.

This would have been a prime moment for lanes to be broken. HLC staff could have gone to Shaffer to have him tell Benekiva, "As your customer and investor, we told you we need this. It's holding things up. Just do it."

Benekiva could have just as easily asked Shaffer to fix this by saying, "To protect your investment, you need to step in tell your team they can't have these things so we can deliver first revenue and meet our next milestone."

Neither of these things happened.

Instead, the Benekiva team worked to fully understand the requirements, their impact on the business, and why they were being positioned as critical. What they found is that the consultant was the sole source of that push, which was lengthening the project, and hence the consultant's contract. This was not a case of delivery failure or scope creep. Instead, it was a case of misaligned incentives where HLC and Benekiva wanted a functionally viable delivery as quickly as possible, and the consultant wanted the project to go as long as possible since their pay was based on their time on the project. That's not to imply the consultant did this consciously or maliciously, but their incentives (payment for length of time worked) would inherently reward them for slower or extended delivery and punish them if delivery was faster. That is, someone whose work was around getting the project to successful completion was not being incentivized for that outcome, and therefore ended up working against it.

With this information in hand, the founders sat down with Shaffer for their quarterly investment and strategy meeting. Rather than being about either side strongarming the other or asking for a favor, it was a clear, fact-based discussion of the project's progress (or lack thereof) and drivers of it. Shaffer was able to use that to make a decision within his business to end the consultant's contract. That would get the project back on track while also giving his team more of a direct relationship with Benekiva to help protect against this issue recurring.

What he did not do was tell his team that this functionality wasn't needed. Nor did he tell Benekiva to find a way to get it done. He removed the barrier to the teams working as they should and let them solve the problem together from there. In the end, both companies agreed this was not a go-live contingency, so they could get back on track with the scope they had originally been focused on.

This was an example of how, by defining the lanes of responsibility in the project and the investment, the two companies empowered their people to work together with those they really needed to rather than just escalating over their heads or working around them. This also helped establish a healthy relationship between the companies.

Benekiva has tried to replicate this with all of their customers and found that it enables them to have a very unique relationship with each customer that they would not otherwise have. They also found it helps them move faster when implementing and provide a solution that delivers more value than they would with a different approach.

This gets at the age-old desire many solution or service providers talk about around not being seen as a vendor, but a partner. In fact, Benekiva takes it a step further where the idea of being a 'partner to' the customer still feels too much like something 'other than' for what they are trying to achieve.

Instead, they want to feel like the two organizations are truly in it together, as part of the same team. Williams said, "We're not vendors. The moment we become vendors; we've lost. We're a *partnership* with our customers, and we want to be known that way."

Being partners in it together really was the way to describe this first customer experience for Benekiva. It gave the founders the real feedback they needed on their idea and their solution. It gave them the financial backing they needed to move forward with their vision yet did so in a way that protects their interests as they build the business.

For Homesteaders, they got the solution they needed, and have seen meaningful benefit from it, easily generating a positive ROI on their role as customer. However, the way they engaged and grew from working together has been yielding what Shaffer had initially hoped for.

> "We're not vendors. The moment we become vendors; we've lost. We're a *partnership* with our customers, and we want to be known that way."
>
> – Brent Williams
> CEO & Co-Founder,
> Benekiva

Benekiva has gone on to strong and rapid success, counting a number of other Life insurers as customers, but also expanding into P&C. They have a customer roster including many Tier 1, household named insurance companies, and, as mentioned above, have nearly 100 people in the company as of early 2023 from that initial start of three, part-timers.

That means Shaffer's insistence on looking at the investment decision around the market potential was clearly the better lens than how to use the investment to bend Benekiva to HLC's will on specific functionality or development decisions. It also means Benekiva is learning so many new and better ways of working, and incorporating those into their solution, which provides additional value to HLC as a customer – none of which would be possible if they had built something just for HLC.

But, perhaps bigger than any of the financial or functional wins, Shaffer looks at how HLC works today, and can point to the impact of this project in starting the momentum of cultural change. The team works differently today, is more collaborative and open to new ways of thinking and is willing to try things that may seem risky through the 115-plus-year-old lens they have historically applied. Homesteaders has replicated what they did with Benekiva with a few other insurtechs now, and those have also been success stories.

The one area where he is not sure how they would react is with a 'failed' project. So far, every chance HLC has taken like they did with Benekiva has worked out well. As Shaffer thinks back to his mentality that even a failure with Benekiva would still make them better off, he hasn't gotten a chance to see how the team would react in that situation, and if they would take the learnings, growth, and benefits as outweighing the idea that things *technically* did not work out.

But he has hope that, if that were to happen, they would see the upside to failure given how they've handled not just the high moments of these projects, but the frustrations and difficulties that are inherent in even the best projects.

The honesty, humility and responsibility that has developed since the early days of the partnership of the two companies clearly shows – not just for Homesteaders, but for Benekiva, too.

Foundations for The Future

- Define the lanes of responsibility within each organization and across them to ensure the right decisions are made in a timely fashion and in a way that does not damage the working relationship of the partners. They may be hard to establish and defend, and doing so only gets harder when an investment is added to the picture. Despite the challenge, the importance of doing it and cost of not having this clarity can be material or even catastrophic.

- Frequent, honest feedback can be critical not only for keeping a project moving in the right direction, but defining how the companies work together and the level of trust and comfort the teams have. This can only come from honest feedback in both directions paired with the humility needed to take in and assimilate the perspectives of others.

- Striking the balance between getting the external help you need and keeping as close a working relationship as possible between insurtechs and insurers can be hard. If outside help is needed, ensure the right incentives are in place so everyone is rowing in the same direction, whether intentionally or subconsciously.

- Working with a startup can be risky, but even if the project fails, there may be benefits that make it all worthwhile – if you are willing to engage free of the rules and constraints of the past. Keep the intangible, company culture benefits top of mind as you decide whether and how to work together to bring about change.

III. COLLABORATING FOR THE FUTURE

Each story here is interesting in its own right, and each has a wealth of lessons we can all benefit from, whether we sit on the carrier side, solution provider side, or somewhere else in the equation. While there is value individually, when we look across the entire collection of cases, we find the strongest lessons we should all endeavor to take into our context to get the most out of every collaborative initiative we face. That could be between insurers and solution providers, as it was here, or it could be amongst teams within a company, or even peers within a team. How we work together at every level of collaboration is critical for the success of our industry today and as the world we operate in continues to change.

And, as with the prior books, none of the lessons here on their own nor all of them combined mean we will necessarily succeed, nor does the lack of them mean we will automatically fail. However, the lessons can be powerful enablers of our success or help protect against failure.

The companies they collaborated with are also wildly different, doing markedly different things. We saw examples of pre-revenue (or even pre-existence) startups through to a publicly listed market leader.

That means anyone thinking their context is too different for these lessons to apply should step back and ask if that's really the case, or if the variety of players here and the way the lessons transcend each of their specific details suggests that they truly do apply to every context out there.

Finally, the insights from these stories don't exist in a vacuum. They come on the back of the findings from the ICI that inspired this work in the first place, reinforcing the broad applicability and impact of the learnings. And they can be built upon the six lessons from the first two *Future of Insurance* books, providing a wealth of guidance for anyone looking to innovate and evolve.

Looking across the rich insights in the stories in this book, three consistent lessons rise to the top for us all as overarching Foundations for the Future to take forward:
1. Make Fast, Rational Decisions
2. Be on The Same Team
3. Respect The Lanes of Responsibility

We will look at each of these in turn in this final section of the book, starting with the power of making fast, rational decisions.

9. Make Fast, Rational Decisions

This industry is not known for speed. We are, after all, a risk averse industry, and that means we often take our time to study options, discuss them, and run them through extensive decision-making protocols and pathways. While that can serve to protect us from some failures, it can also protect us from some successes. It can also make working with us frustrating.

When it comes to seeing projects through to fruition, the speed with which we make decisions can directly lead to missed delivery timing. It can also lead to budget overruns or scope reductions because our failure to be decisive creates a domino of negative impacts to delivery or leads us down a path of less-than-optimal choices with cascading ramifications.

Making decisions quickly isn't quite good enough, though. You must make *the right decisions* quickly. And that can be hard, especially when it may seem risky or like too much of a change from how we've worked in the past. Here, we need to remember why we embarked on the project in question, and whether one of the choices we're deciding about is driven by politics, discomfort, unfamiliarity or another form of insecurity or negative impactors of judgment. Every decision has tradeoffs between costs and benefits. We need to rationally and clearly disassociate emotion-driven, reactionary choices from the right path to take. That could mean some people involved are unhappy or unsupportive, but, frankly, that's a sign of a need for cultural change that is much bigger than any one decision you will need to make. Absent that change, you will repeatedly be pushed to make sub-optimal decisions to placate people rather than make ideal decisions to seize the opportunity in front of you.

While Nationwide and Kinetic's story spanned multiple years before they were in market with the MGA offering, it was actually a story of clear decisiveness and speed. From the initial meeting to investing, Nationwide moved fast, though that was still long before an insurance partnership bore fruit.

Brian Anderson stayed engaged after investing, helping to introduce Kinetic to the Workers Compensation team, and steward a pilot effort with an insured. Staying engaged allowed Anderson and the Ventures team to help get the right decision makers involved and use the diligence behind the investment decision to help manage some potential drivers of slow down as the business started to consider working with Kinetic.

With the pilot not generating the kind of results either side was hoping for – it was fine, but not a clear winner – the two companies could have limped on together, looking for other pilot opportunities rather than give up on the sunk cost of designing the pilot approach, putting the time into what a partnership could look like, or potentially weakening the investment the Ventures team had made into Kinetic.

Instead, they made the rational decision not to consider any sunk costs or fear looking like they were admitting defeat and let Kinetic put its efforts into other approaches that might have stronger results. That ended up paying dividends for Kinetic, who found the right market segment to target, and understand how to do so successfully. Without that, it's hard to imagine that the two sides would have come together again on the MGA approach, or that it would have gone as well as it already has.

And to make that MGA partnership a success, both companies worked diligently, creatively and rationally on a number of fronts. They sorted out what needed to be done by which side (e.g., who would do underwriting and distribution vs. compliance and claims). When they came up against regular decision cadence or priorities at Nationwide, they partnered with those areas to see if there was a path to move faster, safely, and got support from IT, Compliance and others to do so. Without this willingness to keep the project moving at every juncture by Hoppe and the team at Nationwide E&S, Anderson and the Ventures team and Elhawary and the team at Kinetic, they would never have met the goal they set in the summer of 2022 to be writing business by January 2022, let alone going live a month earlier.

Tim Hays raised decision speed specifically in designing the governance and approach for Mountain West's work with Guidewire. He was adamant that they leave Guidewire's code as untouched as possible, and, ideally, completely. That meant the company would repeatedly face moments where people were being asked to change how they worked before, how their product looked, or other shifts that would no doubt leave people uncomfortable and feeling exposed or at risk from a new approach they had never seen work before.

In addition to the guardrails Hays put in place as guiding principles to leave the system as off-the-shelf as possible, he also ensured there were frequent meetings of the major decision makers so no issue or decision could go unresolved more than a few days. Many companies try this sort of weekly or biweekly meeting cadence, and soon find people treating it as an optional meeting they can prioritize other things over. With the full support of CEO Geesey, Hays was able to ensure all the necessary people were at the table every time they met. This ensured complete debate from all perspectives, and that every decision could be shared with the business with the knowledge and support of the leader responsible for the impacted area.

Hays started with a monthly steering committee meeting after initially recognizing that a quarterly cadence would be far too slow for a project that would only span a year. While monthly meetings are more frequent than many companies use, Mountain West and Guidewire saw the need for even greater speed and moved to weekly meetings to protect the forward momentum even more.

> "How do you go fast? Stop doing the things that make you go slow."
>
> – Tim Hays
> VP & CIO, Mountain West Farm Bureau Insurance

As Hays said, "How do you go fast? Stop doing the things that make you go slow." Through living that on this project, Mountain West has not only captured huge leverage from their Guidewire implementation, but moved their internal culture on how they make decisions and their willingness to push themselves on which path to take, even if it feels uncomfortable or unfamiliar.

Ohio Mutual and Pinpoint showed both sides of the decision-making coin. Initially, while both companies were interested, the direction for what to do wasn't clear, making it hard for either to be decisive. OMIG had already structured itself in such a way as to move quickly on new initiatives, and Pinpoint, being a startup, was ready and able to be nimble. But without a clear goal, it is hard to know what you're deciding on regardless of how frequently you try to make decisions. That is, while they could make the right decision quickly, they didn't know what the definition of 'right' was in the first place.

That all changed when a target for their efforts emerged, and the two sides moved quickly. Ohio Mutual had removed a major impedance to speed in the contracting of a proof of concept with their NDA+, meaning the companies could keep moving ahead instead of being stuck negotiating terms for an initial effort. Sometimes the fastest decision making is actually to remove the need for it in the first place, and that's exactly what OMIG did.

When the proof of concept showed the value of the solution, Ohio Mutual did not waste time deciding to move forward. They had a success criteria defined in the PoC, exceeded it, and therefore had what they needed to move to the next step without excessive deliberation. This is a common stalling point where you end up in a PoC loop because, despite defining the gate to moving ahead, uncertainty and insecurity can set in after a PoC or pilot, leading to a seemingly unending series of questions that need to be answered, only to be followed by new questions. OMIG defined success for the PoC and stood by that definition when it had been met, allowing them to move forward without re-adjudicating the idea of working with Pinpoint.

The two sides still needed to work out the commercial terms, and that did prove to require more debate and discussion, but they made a point to do so frequently and with all the right parties involved so they didn't run the risk of that process impacting their ability to move forward when they both knew it made sense.

This proved especially important since OMIG essentially had one annual window to implement Pinpoint's solution, summertime. If contracting was allowed to stretch too long, they'd miss the chance to kick off the process for another year, potentially exposing the company to additional premium leakage and covering losses it should not have covered. And, more importantly to OMIG and their agents, insureds could be at risk of serious loss or even death that could have been prevented by the right intervention.

AEIG's work with Protosure is one of frequent, rational decisions. Neumann called out their ability to do this because of their size and ownership structure, where they choose to make decisions based on economic value, and to do so quickly so that they can start to capture that value as soon as possible. Yet it's important to realize that any company can choose to do that, regardless of structure. Protosure has seen that firsthand through one of their current customers, which is one of the largest global insurers, with over $35 billion in premium.

For Protosure, their solution itself is about not having to make decisions due to the simplicity and ease with which it can be deployed. They engineered their solution to allow customers to self-deploy and use it easily, again looking to the path of not having to make decisions at all as a way to speed decision making. By removing so many points of trade-off or decision in an implementation, Protosure inherently makes the process of negotiating terms and going live easier because there are fewer nodes on the decision tree you would navigate because of their approach.

Homesteaders Life and Benekiva, by having both investment and commercial deployment relationships, could have gone twice as slow because of the nuanced layers of decisions and opinions introduced. Like Mountain West and Guidewire, the two companies relied on frequent meetings throughout the project, but also ensured the people in those discussions were empowered to do what was needed. As we saw in the case, when people tried to go up the chain to Shaffer to step in, he pushed both sides to work together to sort it out. That might have been slower than him just making a call in that moment, but it would not have broken down any remaining barriers to decision speed between the companies going forward.

They used frequent and well-defined meetings with explicit decision-making authority to keep things moving and get to the right outcome. The one break they had from this was in the issue with the outside consultant slowing down the project by creating emotion around an issue that was trivial, if not irrelevant. Having the consultant sit between HLC's team and Benekiva only served to slow and complicate decision making. Once that was recognized by both sides, they moved quickly to have more direct discussion and decision making on the project.

Shaffer wanted to work with Benekiva not just for the solution they'd get, or the investment returns they could earn, but for what it could mean for HLC's culture and operation. He's seen the impact this has had on how his functions work together internally and with other outside partners, their willingness to do things differently, and the speed they're now willing and able to move at.

It seems obvious that making decisions slowly or for the wrong reasons will lead a project off course and rob of us all that could have been if we did things better. Yet this is one of the most common issues in any collaboration I've seen and is tied to the second most important issue raised in the ICI around how companies navigate the problems they face and bring them to resolution. That means, while obvious, there is both a lot of room for us all to do better, and the payback for doing better is huge.

When you face having to wait for a key meeting, ask if there's a way to bring the decision forward. When there's a push to choose a path of "how we've always done things" or when politics is behind a choice (even if it benefits you), ask how to navigate deciding what to do absent that influence. It will speed the project up, increase the benefits of the work and help to redefine what's possible for your organization.

10. Be on The Same Team

It should come as no surprise that, the more you reinforce the separation of companies (or departments in the same company), the less collaborative the effort will feel. And you will suffer for it. The better the working dynamic and the alignment of goals between everyone involved an any effort, the more likely it is to bear fruit.

This is a moment some of you may want to raise a concern or consideration around blurring the lines between contractor or supplier and employee. You may be thinking, "If we treat them like part of the company, then they can sue for benefits."

While that *could* be true, this is a prime example of the kind of risk aversion we often fall back on to justify working in a less productive, collaborative way. And treating a supplier like they're part of the project team does not mean you start crossing lines of employment practices like extending employee benefits such as time off, meal perks or other things to them. It means not talking in the project of "us" and "them". It means including your partners in critical conversations with all the necessary details and information flowing freely. It means being willing to roll up your sleeves and do your part in the project as much as you expect them to do their part.

Nationwide and Kinetic benefitted in their commercial relationship from the level of connection the companies already had through their investment relationship, and the openness Kinetic had already established with Nationwide around the details of their strategy, operation and performance. That allowed the Ventures team to vouch for Kinetic internally on a number of fronts to help bring comfort in the business with the idea of partnering with Kinetic.

It also extended to how Brian Anderson treated other parts of Nationwide as he tried to help Kinetic navigate the path to going live with their MGA model. Rather than engaging with IT or other teams as somehow subservient to or in service of the investment Nationwide had made in Kinetic, he brought them into the fold to try to help deliver on the goals of the partnership while also respecting their autonomy and right to not be able to help in the way Anderson was hoping they would. That is, he engaged with them as equals critical to the success of the project.

While Mountain West and Guidewire clearly had different responsibilities throughout their work together, Hays was very clear from the start that there would be no abdicating responsibility to a vendor, and Mountain West's people had to be involved every step of the way. This was true internally, where people from the business had to be directly involved and integrated into the project rather than letting IT represent them. This was also the case in how IT worked with Guidewire, where Hays insisted Mountain West's people presented demos to the business users rather than seeing that as a 'vendor' responsibility.

Hays shared the impact of this in the level of responsibility his team felt for the code, even when it was as off-the-shelf as they were able to keep it. The level of line-blurring between the business, IT and Guidewire helped the Mountain West team seemingly feel as much ownership, understanding and responsibility for the new system as they would if they had fully-built the code in-house.

This paid dividends when the project started to fall behind, with both companies working together to find ways to get it back on track, and never falling to finger pointing or blaming because there was no sense of one side doing something to the other. All the players were moving in lock step, got to that difficult place together, and could only emerge from it by working together.

For Guidewire, it was clear that they weren't just serving Mountain West, but deeply connected to the strategic value of their work as if it was their own business they were unlocking potential for. In talking to them, Guidewire's team was clearly excited by what Mountain West had enabled through the project, and what that could mean for the business going forward.

It was almost hard to tell which company people worked for given the ownership and pride they felt for what both companies contributed.

Ohio Mutual's use of their NDA+ approach was another example of this mentality. NDAs are meant to bring down walls of secrecy so two organizations can speak freely about potentially sensitive or proprietary details that could be necessary in their work together. OMIG knew an NDA would not be strong enough to share the kind of data Pinpoint needed to perform a proof of value, yet also knew that engaging in a full-scale contract to get to that point could be onerous for both companies, create potential conflict early on, and slow both companies from getting the initial indication that it was worth the effort to move ahead. By taking a pragmatic and collaborative approach to protecting their data without introducing additional factors prematurely, OMIG allowed things to move ahead while progressively fostering the building of a relationship with Pinpoint. That took an inherent level of trust on OMIG's part, which is hard to do when you see the other side almost as an adversary in negotiating a deal.

This repeated itself when it came time to sign a commercial agreement between the companies. Both companies had considerations that were important to them that might make a traditional approach difficult to agree to.

OMIG did not want to face steep upfront implementation costs given their scale and the uncertainty that still remained even after the PoC. Pinpoint, being an early-stage startup, couldn't risk compromising so much to fit OMIG's implementation cost concern that they ended up with a long-term contract that was not economically viable for them or, worse yet, threatened the company's viability.

That meant a more flexible, shared value approach would be necessary, but still left the question of the structure, triggers, and economics. While the spirit of it gave both sides skin in the game and protection, defining the specifics would still be difficult. The two companies focused on the intention rather than anchoring on any given numbers, and worked together on the economic model that would underly it, making it easier to agree to the structure since they built it together instead of just going back and forth on opposing numbers for each variable. That is, they developed the logic together as a team, allowing everyone to move forward with understanding and agreement at the foundational level of the structure rather than disagreeing on any individual point one side proposed or stood firm on.

Internally, OMIG's decision to work collaboratively with their outside counsel, as if they were part of the project team and company itself, meant contracting was smoother and redlining was more productive because everyone involved understood the purpose of their efforts.

Protosure and AEIG enjoyed a healthy camaraderie from the start, fueled by the straight-forward, results-focused evaluation AEIG's leadership was willing to do when looking at Protosure. That inherently cut out a lot of the natural barriers to feeling connected and collaborative across the companies. But this extended to the way they worked together, with Breuer and the Protosure team communicating freely and frequently. And when they felt they needed even easier ways to communicate, they moved to Slack, where Breuer and AEIG could communicate with the Protosure team the same way the startup was communicating internally already. That was a minor shift from email to instant messaging and chat, but it also removed a symbolic divide between client and provider that helped them move even faster.

With Benekiva, it has always been a goal to really be part of the team at any carrier they work with. While they were generally working closely with HLC's project team, there was a complication. A single person acting as a layer between the companies was enough to create friction and separation that impacted the project. With the consultant removed from the equation, the teams got even more integrated, and the project quickly got back on track.

For Shaffer, had he stepped in to force an answer on his people or Benekiva, that would have instantly reinforced any sense of separation between the teams rather than fostering a closer working relationship. Instead, he removed the barrier, but let them work together to find the actual resolution, giving them all a chance to rebuild the relationship fully to support how they worked together going forward.

It may have been easier to just make a decision on whether to develop the functionality in question or stop worrying about it, but doing so would have had far greater costs over the life of the project than would be saved by making an immediate decision, and Shaffer recognized the benefit to the working relationship in the path he chose.

Being part of the same team is a feeling more than anything explicit. It comes from the sum of individual moments, interactions and actions taken over the life of the project. It comes from how you bring two cultures together, what working styles one side imposes on the other, and how well everyone reads the room and adjusts to develop more and more comfort along the way.

It can be easy to forget that there's as much at stake for the customer as there is for the supplier if things don't work out (or, potentially, far more). Just like the advice we've all heard that, when you're applying for a job, you're interviewing them as much as they are interviewing you, we need to remember that two organizations working together will both need to adjust and flex to get what they're hoping to from the other side.

11. Respect The Lanes of Responsibility

It may seem obvious that each company, and the people in them, would have specific roles and responsibilities in any project. Yet we so often see moments where things can get blurred, and the impact that blurring has on the project's success.

For Nationwide and Kinetic, there was an obvious need to spell out the responsibilities in their MGA relationship around things like underwriting, distribution, claims and compliance. Since Nationwide has such a strong existing distribution footprint, I assumed Kinetic would want to leverage that in launching their MGA. In fact, the opposite was true as Kinetic had learned a lot through their work with self-insured customers in identifying what makes a good risk and how to properly onboard them. The team felt it was critical therefore that they build out their own broker relationships to be sure the channel would be built to effectively support this new approach to Workers Compensation insurance. Equally important to Kinetic was that Nationwide be able to support the effort with their Claims and Compliance capabilities – things Kinetic lacked and knew they couldn't build out quickly enough for their needs.

Internally at Nationwide, Anderson also respected the responsibility of IT to prioritize the projects in front of them, even if that meant the Kinetic launch may not happen when they wanted it to. His respect for IT's responsibility for *its* priorities was part of what allowed for the kind of partnership building that found solutions to potential barriers to meeting their go-live goal of January 2022.

Mountain West's Tim Hays' insistence that his people be 'on the keyboard' during system demos and releases to establish their responsibility for the system in the long term was critical. He had seen too many instances where a lack of internal responsibility led to failures that were blamed on vendors only to be repeated because people wouldn't take the lessons from those failures since they didn't feel responsibility.

As Hays said, "Asking if the vendor will keep you on track is the wrong question. It's *your* project. If it succeeds or fails, it's *your* fault Own your fate and deliver to it."

Pinpoint had a strong feeling that OMIG would get value from avoiding fire losses through their work together. They raised this to OMIG when working on the shared value model, but OMIG pushed back. While it is possible that losses would improve, it was not possible to tie that explicitly to the new prediction model being deployed. Just because someone has a wood burning stove does not mean their house will burn down, so it is possible there just didn't happen to be any fires that year. Equally possible is that surprise fires could still occur despite these efforts, but that does not necessarily mean the initiative was a failure or Pinpoint should be penalized. There's no way to know how many fires would have occurred without these efforts, so it isn't possible to establish a baseline to look to for savings from the work.

While Pinpoint's model may reduce the number of home fires for Ohio Mutual, they had to follow OMIG's lead on whether to consider this in their value calculations because OMIG is responsible for underwriting these risks. This wasn't a point of contention or negotiation for the two companies since Pinpoint respected that this was in Ohio Mutual's lane.

Protosure had built a solution that their clients can truly run with, without needing to call on Protosure every time they want to deploy a new product or make a change. Despite not having worked that way before, AEIG embraced that approach, seeing what responsibility they had been empowered with by the tool they were using. They were able to add another product themselves, without involving Protosure, because they knew they had the responsibility *and* capability to do it. That allowed them to move faster and get further benefit and value from the solution they had put in place.

Benekiva's leadership talked about lanes of responsibility extensively in how they built and run the company. But it's an equally strong lesson in the success of their dual relationship with HLC. At any time in their role as customer, HLC could have leveraged their position as investor to their benefit. Shaffer could have dictated what Benekiva needed to build as their sole investor. He could have heard things his team wanted and pushed Benekiva to do it.

Similarly, he could have been approached by his team about something they wanted and told them to give up on that request because it wasn't good for their investment in Benekiva.

And he could have placed himself on the project sponsorship committee to ensure he was in control of both the investment and customer interactions and decision making.

Instead, he realized the conflict, and the potential risk to both outcomes HLC was focused on – getting a great new system and making a wise investment. But it was his other goal – seeing HLC evolve culturally – that likely helped most in keeping him from stepping into either side of the relationship with his interests from the other side. Like how he navigated the issue with the consultant, Shaffer had to let people maintain their responsibilities and see them through if he wanted his team to change in the way they have.

This can be an area of particular difficulty in the coming together of startups and established companies. At startups, because things are moving so fast and there's so much to do, people's official responsibilities are often a mere fraction of what they actually work on every day. And when you step up and do something beyond your immediate role to help, it's generally appreciated (or simply expected).

In established companies, there are usually far more defined roles and responsibilities, as well as perceived negative outcomes for those who overstep in many organizations.

This can mean startup staff on a project can become frustrated by customer staff who don't seem to be stepping up, pitching in, or are content to leave something undone when it's someone else's responsibility – even if the project suffers for it. It can also mean customer staff are confused by who to go to for something or may even be offended or feel pressured by being asked to do things they're not responsible for.

Navigating this can be tricky, but it's not impossible. In fact, whether there are aligned senses of responsibility across the companies or not, there's value in clarifying upfront who is responsible for what, and how to navigate issues around that, like escalation points. This is a key input into the critical factor of Issue Resolution we saw in the

ICI where having pre-defined clarity on where to turn can help resolve problems that arise.

It's important to remember how the Benekiva team talked about the idea of lanes of responsibility. It's not that you cannot have thoughts, opinions, or input into something outside of your lane. It's just that there is someone who technically 'owns' that space and will have the final say. And when they do, you agree to support that decision knowing you were able to raise your thoughts to be considered along the way.

12. Evolving Ahead

This book being less about the trends or direction of innovation means there's less of an automatic discussion of what's to come in terms of technology, product, customer experience, etc.

Instead, the future-looking message here is one that has been discussed in the past two books, but from a different angle, and it's in the title of the book itself – collaboration.

The last two books talked about how insurtech and legacy carriers aren't likely to put the other out of business but will come together to move the industry forward. That could be through acquisition or partnership, or simply by pushing each other to do new things or old things in a better way through the mechanism of healthy competition.

Before I share my thoughts, I had an idea. What is the biggest discussion point in the industry today, or perhaps technology at large? The answer is AI, but even more specifically, ChatGPT. So, I decided it would be interesting to see what ChatGPT thinks of the future path of legacy insurers and insurtechs.

So, I asked ChatGPT, "How will legacy insurers and insurtech startups work together in the future?" The following is how ChatGPT sees the path ahead:

> Legacy insurers and insurtech startups will likely work together in the future in several ways, as each brings unique strengths to the table. Here are a few potential ways that collaboration could take place:
> 1. Partnerships: Insurtech startups often bring innovative technology and digital capabilities, while legacy insurers have extensive industry expertise and established customer bases. By partnering with one another, both parties can benefit from the strengths of the other. For example, an

insurtech startup might provide an insurance platform or mobile app, while the legacy insurer provides the underwriting and claims management.
2. Acquisitions: Some legacy insurers may choose to acquire promising insurtech startups that complement their existing businesses. This can help them to quickly gain new technology or expand their offerings to customers.
3. Investments: Legacy insurers may also invest in insurtech startups, providing funding to help them grow and develop. In exchange, they may gain access to new technologies or innovative business models that they can integrate into their own operations.
4. Collaborative Innovation: Legacy insurers may also work with insurtech startups to create new products or services that better meet the needs of customers. By combining the knowledge and expertise of both parties, they can create innovative solutions that neither could develop on their own.

Overall, the key to successful collaboration between legacy insurers and insurtech startups will be finding ways to leverage each other's strengths to create value for customers. As the insurance industry continues to evolve, we can expect to see more partnerships, acquisitions, and investments that bring these two groups together.[6]

That is not earth shattering, nor is it at risk of becoming a meme about the absurdity of some ChatGPT responses. It's rational, reasonable, and plausible. It's also not very descriptive, specific or predictive.

But I think it's still right.

In the spirit of healthy competition, I asked Google Bard the same question and got a very similar response, but with a notable twist. Bard listed similar ways to work together as ChatGPT, but called out the specific mechanisms both sides of the equation could benefit from, and then took a turn to focus even more on collaboration. It said:

---

[6] ChatGPT, personal communication, April 5, 2023.

The future of the insurance industry is likely to be characterized by even more collaboration between legacy insurers and insurtech startups. As the insurance industry continues to evolve, both legacy insurers and insurtech startups will need to be willing to work together in order to succeed.

Here are some of the benefits of collaboration between legacy insurers and insurtech startups:

- Increased innovation: Legacy insurers can benefit from the innovative ideas and technologies that insurtech startups are developing. Insurtech startups can benefit from the resources and expertise that legacy insurers have to offer.
- Reduced costs: Legacy insurers can reduce costs by outsourcing certain tasks to insurtech startups. Insurtech startups can reduce costs by leveraging the economies of scale that legacy insurers have to offer.
- Improved customer service: Legacy insurers can improve customer service by partnering with insurtech startups that are experts in customer experience. Insurtech startups can improve customer service by partnering with legacy insurers that have a large customer base.
- Increased market share: Legacy insurers can increase market share by partnering with insurtech startups that are experts in new markets. Insurtech startups can increase market share by partnering with legacy insurers that have a strong brand reputation.

Overall, collaboration between legacy insurers and insurtech startups is a win-win situation for both parties. By working together, they can achieve things that they would not be able to achieve on their own.[7]

Without me using the word 'collaboration', Bard went deep on the idea, and all there is to gain from it. And it's spot on.

I then asked ChatGPT the question that's been bubbling around since the early days of InsurTech – who will win, the startups or the legacy insurers?

Specifically, I asked, "Will startup insurtechs put legacy insurers out of business?" To which, it answered:

---

[7] Google Bard, personal communication, April 10, 2023.

It is unlikely that startup insurtechs will put legacy insurers out of business. While insurtechs are disrupting the insurance industry with innovative technologies and business models, legacy insurers have decades of experience, established brands, and a loyal customer base that insurtechs may not have.

Furthermore, many legacy insurers are adapting to the changing market conditions by investing in technology, collaborating with insurtech startups, and launching their own digital platforms. They are also taking advantage of their existing infrastructure and distribution networks to offer a more personalized and seamless customer experience.

That said, insurtechs are forcing legacy insurers to innovate and evolve, which is ultimately good for the industry and consumers. The competition from insurtechs is pushing legacy insurers to become more customer-centric, reduce costs, and adopt new technologies. This is leading to greater efficiency and better products and services for consumers.

In summary, while insurtechs are disrupting the industry, it is unlikely that they will put legacy insurers out of business. Instead, the two will likely continue to coexist and work together to offer the best products and services to consumers.[8]

Again, even when I pressed the issue more directly, ChatGPT fell back on the idea of collaboration, bringing more weight to the premise of this book.

For fairness, I asked Bard that question, as well, and got another take on the symbiotic relationship that will prevail rather than one of winners and losers. Bard said:

It is unlikely that insurtech startups will put legacy insurers out of business altogether. However, they are likely to have a significant impact on the industry, and some legacy insurers may not be able to adapt to the changing landscape.

Insurtech startups are disrupting the insurance industry in a number of ways. They are using new technologies to make insurance more efficient and affordable. They are also developing

---

[8] ChatGPT, personal communication, April 5, 2023.

new products and services that meet the needs of a changing customer base.

Legacy insurers are facing a number of challenges in the face of insurtech competition. They need to invest in new technologies and develop new products and services in order to stay competitive. They also need to change their culture and become more agile in order to respond to the changing needs of customers.

Some legacy insurers will be able to adapt to the changing landscape and thrive in the new era of insurtech. However, others may not be able to make the necessary changes and will be forced to exit the market.

The future of the insurance industry is likely to be characterized by a mix of legacy insurers and insurtech startups. The legacy insurers that are able to adapt to the changing landscape will be able to coexist with the insurtech startups and continue to provide insurance to customers.[9]

So, while they both did well, I feel like Bard went further, and got to more of the dynamics at play. But it says something that they said very aligned things and clearly agree on what's to come.

As for me, I do think that both legacy and insurtech insurers will continue to exist, with neither putting the other out of business. Sure, individual players may come and go, but I don't think the startups will disrupt all traditional insurers out of existence. Nor do I think legacy carriers will out-compete every startup in every area, ensuring their failure.

Instead, I think more and more situations where the two work together will arise. That may take the form of partnership, where a startup may be well-positioned to serve a particular market segment or channel more effectively than an incumbent, so the two collaborate to add the incumbent's resources to the startup's positioning, resulting in a better overall solution than either could have built alone.

It may take the form of an acquisition, which could go in either direction, giving the assets and capabilities of the acquired company the chance to be applied in a new way. While they're both insurtechs, Metromile was much older than Lemonade, yet Lemonade was the acquirer, benefitting from Metromile's richer historical data to fuel

---

[9] Google Bard, personal communication, April 10, 2023.

underwriting decisions as they moved into Auto. The story is too early to know how it will play out, but Metromile added something Lemonade would not have been able to do themselves, or at least not for a long time.

In the opposite direction, Allstate's acquisition of Esurance years ago, the granddaddy of insurtech startups, brought a totally new approach to distribution than Allstate had been using, as well as a leaner approach to innovation and operation. While it's since been folded into the Allstate brand, Esurance added to Allstate's capabilities, approach and overall story in a way the legacy carrier likely could not have achieved alone.

We have seen non-carrier acquisitions, like USAA buying Noblr, bringing telematics capabilities in-house for USAA. Travelers bought Simply Business to access the direct, digital distribution market for small business insureds, which they could not easily do with their existing distribution model given the channel conflict issues.

We also see insurtechs acquiring capabilities, like Next's purchase of Juniper Labs and AP Intego or At-bay's purchase of Relay.

Whether insurtechs being the acquirer or target, and whether the target is an insurer or solution provider, there are clear examples of players coming together to achieve something they couldn't do on their own. And, of course, it does not have to be achieved through acquisition, with hundreds or even thousands of deals being announced every year where companies partner, or services are purchased to seize on a new opportunity or overcome a barrier.

In the stories in this book, whether the insurer is new or old, the collaboration is about working with solution and service providers to enhance and evolve what we do and how we do it. But it's still about collaboration. The story looking ahead, though, is one of appetite.

While we have made progress in many areas of how we engage with others, I still see the majority of efforts hampered by a pace of business and insistence on process almost for process's sake. I recently watched an MGA wait through five months of underwriting committee meetings at their reinsurer to get approval because key decision makers decided not to attend the meeting, or because people forgot what was discussed before and couldn't be bothered to review the papers before the meeting each time, forcing the capacity decision to be put off another month. And now that approval has been granted, the capacity provider continues to ask new questions that are not actually relevant to the lines of business involved, keeping the MGA from writing yet.

That example is certainly not an anomaly, or unique to capacity arrangements. I regularly see carriers who decide they want to move forward with a new solution still take months to get contracts sorted out, set timelines, assign resources and more.

We have to be willing to do better, and not accept or justify ways we've worked in the past that slow things down. That's the underlying impetus for this book, and that is the fuel for the Future of Insurance.

ACKNOWLEDGMENTS

I want to give a huge thanks to the people from the companies discussed in this book for the time, energy and honesty they gave to the project. Some names appear in the text, and some were behind the scenes but no less valuable and deserve recognition. They are Brian Anderson, Dale Hoppe and Jarrett Dunbar from Nationwide; Haytham Elhawary from Kinetic; Chad Combs, Ryan Ward, Christina Roderick and Todd Boyer from Ohio Mutual; Avi Tuschman, Shannon Shallcross Scott Ham, and Nicohle Schluender from Pinpoint Predictive; Tim Hays from Mountain West Farm Bureau; Christina Colby, Joe Scinto, Guru Venkataramu, Carrie Burns, Deb Pugatch, Brian Desmond and Mike Rosenbaum from Guidewire; Schlomo Neumann from American European Insurance Group; Urijah Kaplan from Protosure; Steve Shaffer from Homesteaders Life; and Brent Williams, Bobbie Shrivastav and Sov en Shrivastav from Benekiva. I also want to thank Sabine VanderLinden for the thought and time she put into writing the foreword – she truly went over and above.

There's a foundational thanks to the concept for this book that goes to David Gritz and Tony Lew, co-founders of InsurTech NY. David and Tony approached me in the height of the pandemic to join an effort they were leading to discover what makes for better or worse collaboration between carriers and solution providers that would become the Insurance Collaboration Index. They assembled a fantastic team who volunteered their time to bring the idea to reality, do the research and find the insights. Alan Walters, Cynthia Hardy, Krishnan Venkatachalam, Mark Gardella, Irene Yang, Roi Hansraj and Mike Fitzgerald were there doing the work, coming together every two weeks for roughly a year, trying to move this noble cause forward. Without that work, this book would not exist. And David Gritz went a step further, contributing his own words, experience and guidance to this book to help make it as rich and impactful as possible.

And to the many companies that I worked with to try unsuccessfully to bring their stories into the book, thank you for what you shared, the efforts you made to try to get your partners or legal teams on board, and the support you showed for the project even when it turned out not to be possible to share your stories. While I can't name most of the insurers who fall into this category, I will recognize solution providers Hover, HOMEE, Carpe Data, Snapsheet, Longitude6 and CCC for their interest and efforts. I would just say these are companies committed to building great partnerships with and results for the insurers they work with, and I would have loved to share the insights they've learned from their experience with many great insurers.

As for the insurers who didn't make the final book, I want to specifically thank Zurich North America who worked diligently to make one of their stories come to life in the book on a very tight timeline. Ultimately, we couldn't do it in time for publication, but their efforts to innovate and commitment to a partnership approach globally deserve recognition. Look for episodes of The Future of Insurance podcast featuring Zurich and some of their partners to hear a small sample of what they've done, and how it's gone.

Lastly, most importantly, and as I do in every one of these books, I must thank you, the readers. To choose to read a book about insurance says something about your commitment to the work you do, the purpose of the industry, and your personal desire to help the industry move forward. Without that attitude, energy, and action, we would fail in our mission to protect the world from risk so dreams can be pursued.

ABOUT THE AUTHORS

Bryan Falchuk is a best-selling author, speaker and consultant to the Insurance industry on the subjects of innovation and change as the Founder and Managing Partner of Insurance Evolution Partners. He is also the President & CEO of The Property & Liability Resource Bureau (PLRB), which supports the U.S. P&C Insurance industry in the delivery of coverage to insureds.

Bryan has been named to several lists of leading voices on innovation in Insurance and InsurTech. He has written for many top publications such as Inc. Magazine, The Chicago Tribune, LA Times and more, been a guest on hundreds of podcasts and radio shows, frequent keynote speaker at industry events, and has presented several TEDx Talks. Bryan has written multiple best-selling books, including *Do a Day* and *The 50 75 100 Solution: Build Better Relationships*, which have won numerous awards and, more importantly, continue to help people change their lives for the better, every day. His best-selling *Future of Insurance* series features case studies of different players in Insurance helping to move the industry forward at a time of disruption, change and opportunity.

Bryan spent over twenty years in the Insurance industry where he was most recently Head of Claims for Hiscox USA before joining AI-enabled InsurTech communications provider Hi Marley to help drive their growth. With his unique experience at both carriers and InsurTechs, after Hi Marley he started IEP, where he brings his perspective to bear to help the industry evolve. Prior to Hiscox, Bryan held leadership roles in corporate strategy, operations and distribution at Liberty Mutual, Beazley and Coverys, and served as a management consultant in McKinsey & Company's Insurance practice.

Bryan holds an MBA from the Tuck School of Business at Dartmouth College and a BA in Economics from Bowdoin College. Learn more about Bryan at bryanfalchuk.com, and follow him on social media at @bryanfalchuk.

David Gritz is a venture capitalist, InsurTech community leader, and InsurTech advisor. He has been a featured speaker at conferences including InsureTech Connect, InsurTech Insights, DigIn, and Reuters Future of Insurance.

David serves as the Managing Director of InsurTech Fund and InsurTech NY (insurtechny.com). InsurTech NY is the largest InsurTech community in North America. It helps insurers connect to high-potential startups through a Global InsurTech Competition, a growth-stage accelerator, and an MGA Lab.

Previously, David served as the Director of Innovation for the Silicon Valley Insurance Accelerator (SVIA) and co-founded Zero, a behavioral safety focused InsurTech acquired by EverestRe. He holds a J.D. from the Mitchell Hamline School of Law and business and industrial engineering degrees from Lehigh University.

Subscribe to The Future of Insurance Podcast
future-of-insurance.com/podcast

Get Updates on The FOI Series
future-of-insurance.com/updates

Connect with Bryan Falchuk
Web: bryanfalchuk.com
LinkedIn: linkedin.com/in/bryanfalchuk
Facebook: facebook.com/bryanfalchuk
Instagram: instagram.com/bryanfalchuk
Twitter: twitter.com/bryanfalchuk

Also by Bryan Falchuk
The Future of Insurance: From Disruption to Evolution, Volume I. The Incumbents
The Future of Insurance: From Disruption to Evolution, Volume II. The Startups
The Future of ESG in Insurance
The Future of Auto Insurance: Connected, Embedded, Subscribed
Unlocking Casualty Results with APD Science
Do a Day: How to Live a Better Life Every Day
The 50 75 100 Solution: Build Better Relationships

Connect with Insurance Evolution Partners
Web: insurance-evolution.com
Facebook: facebook.com/insureevolve
LinkedIn: linkedin.com/company/insureevolve
Instagram: instagram.com/insureevolve
Twitter: twitter.com/insureevolve

Connect with InsurTech NY
Web: insurtechny.com
LinkedIn: linkedin.com/company/insurtechny
Twitter: twitter.com/insurtechny

Made in the USA
Middletown, DE
19 September 2024

60750723R00096